Teaching English: Step by Step

1

Written by Elizabeth Weal
Illustrated by Anastasia Ionkin

Tenaya Press
Palo Alto, CA

For ESL teachers and tutors everywhere

All inquiries should be addressed to
Elizabeth Weal
Tenaya Press
3481 Janice Way
Palo Alto, CA 94303

650-494-3941
ElizabethWeal@tenaya.com

Book design: Stuart Silberman
Cover: Beth Zonderman

About the cover

The cover is a photograph of a portion of a mola. Molas are part of the traditional dress of the Central American Cuna (or Kuna) tribe of the San Blas Islands, a chain of tropical islands along the Atlantic coast of Panama. Molas, which also can be found in Colombia, are hand made using a "reverse appliqué" technique. Several layers of different-colored cloth are sewn together; the design is then formed by cutting parts of each layer away.

ISBN 978-0-9796128-3-1

Contents

A note to teachers

Welcome to *Teaching English: Step by Step 1*, a book that gives teachers and tutors using *Gramática del inglés: Paso a paso 1* and *English Grammar: Step by Step 1* practical speaking and listening activities to accompany the grammar books. The introduction to this book is a personal perspective on teaching English as a Second Language. The remaining chapters follow lockstep with the chapters of the level 1 grammar books. Feel free to copy any and all worksheets!

Acknowledgments

I wrote this book with a few people in mind: Wendy Vasquez, ESL coordinator at Trinity United Methodist Church in Des Moines, Iowa; Martin Steinman, ESL coordinator at the Canal Alliance in San Rafael, CA; Lorraine Reston, ESL teacher at Napa Valley College, in Napa, CA; and Tod Buis, tutor at Partners in English Language Learning in Grass Valley, CA have each in their own way supported my work and encouraged me to forge ahead.

I also want to thank a crack team of editors. Julie Reis reviewed this manuscript from the perspective of an ESL teacher. Phyllis Mayberg did a fine copy editing job and my daughter, Chelsea Hodge, spent much of her Labor Day holiday applying her fine editing skills to the first chapter of the book. Finally, my husband, Bruce Hodge, stepped up to the plate yet again, helping me with countless tasks, from design assistance to 24/7 technical support.

One ESL teacher's perspective

Teacher's Diary

Disneyland

One day, mid-summer vacation, I got a phone call from an administrator at my school asking if I'd be interested in teaching two students who work on an assembly line at a local defense contractor. The teacher who had been teaching the class had had a medical emergency and they needed someone to take her place as soon as possible. It was only a few hours a week, so I readily agreed.

At the first class, we picked up where the other teacher had left off, and so started work on a chapter in the text book on future tense. After 45 minutes or so the book was getting tedious, so I decide to personalize the exercise by asking one of the students about his future plans.

Me: Are you going to have a vacation this year?

Juan: Yes, I'm gong to go to Disneyland.

Me: When are you going to go?

Juan: In September.

Me: Who are you going to go with?

Juan: With my family.

Me: How are you going to get there?

Juan: By car.

Juan did a masterful job--clearly he'd done this before--so we switched to a reading exercise.

The next class we reviewed future tense so I again asked Juan about his vacation plans and he again told me he was going to Disneyland in September.

At the end of the class, I asked Juan whether he would be in class next week, given that it was September and he was planning to go on vacation.

"I made it up," he told me. "No money. My daughter, she go to the university," at which point he proceeded to make a list of the expenses that were coming due that month.

I didn't bring up Disneyland again.

It's no secret that English as a Second Language (ESL) teachers, especially ESL teachers who teach adults, are often regarded as the stepchildren of the teaching profession. It's easy to understand why. What could be easier, the thinking goes, than teaching a skill so ingrained in our brains that it requires not a moment's thought?

After becoming an ESL teacher, I realized how very wrong this conventional wisdom is.

Like many people who teach English to adults, I have no formal training as an ESL teacher. I also have no formal training in grammar other than what I learned in junior high. Thus, I never considered why you say, "I like dancing," but do not say "I like to dancing." Or why you say, "Lucy doesn't have a job" but do not say "Lucy doesn't has a job." That all changed when I got in front of a classroom of students who asked questions like these and I quickly learned that teaching English to adults is not the mental cakewalk many people assume it to be.

A 2006 study by the National Association of Latino Elected and Appointed Officials (NALEO) Educational Fund found that, in cities across the nation, adults interested in taking ESL classes frequently face long waiting lists, crowded classrooms, and other obstacles. In response to these conditions, as well as cuts in state programs which have occurred since that report was issued, more and more churches and grass roots community organizations are offering ESL classes to adults. Many of the people teaching these classes are volunteers who have a passion both for teaching and their students, but who don't necessarily have the time or the inclination to master the nuances of teaching English as a Second Language. It's those teachers who I'm addressing here.

Consider yourself blessed

If you're reading this book, you've probably begun—or are about to begin—pursuing what for me is a true passion: teaching English to immigrants hungry to learn. Lest you think my enthusiasm is a bit over the top, I should tell you that I'm not alone. I met an ESL tutor from Boulder, Colorado who divulged to me that, whenever she gets snippy, her husband insists that she call her tutee to calm her down. A volunteer in Marin County, California, a retired high tech executive, confided to me that teaching a class of twenty English learners was the most rewarding "job" he'd ever had.

I've spent many hours pondering why teaching ESL has such a palliative effect on my psyche. How can it be that however good—or not good—I feel before my class starts, I always feel better when it's over? I've concluded that there are multiple reasons: even if one variable in the equation hasn't kicked in on a particular day, others will have.

The reverence with which my students view me is one factor. My students revere me because I know to put periods at the ends of sentences, can pronounce *beach* so it doesn't sound like *bitch*, and can help them avoid embarrassing situations by correctly distinguishing between *Mr.*, *Miss*, and *Mrs.* For these and similar morsels of basic knowledge I am treated with the esteem normally reserved for Olympians and high priests. I begin handing out scissors and a student is at my elbow, offering to hand them out for me. I arrive to class a few minutes late and the quiets down, not entirely but enough so that it's obvious someone of significance is now in their midst. I relish this respect, and who wouldn't? Yet this is only part of the reason for my exhilaration. A related sentiment is the intense satisfaction that comes from being around students so hungry to learn, analogous, perhaps, to the way a master craftsman might feel amidst a roomful of eager apprentices.

Connecting with other people is what makes us feel human. When I'm teaching ESL, those connections come fast and furious, despite the fact that, at least superficially, my students and I have almost nothing in common. They're mostly house cleaners, prep cooks, and gardeners who spend most of the little free time they have watching TV and playing soccer. I'm a college graduate who rarely watches TV, never plays soccer, and has enough free time to pontificate about why she likes her job.

In all honesty I'm not sure why these connections happen. One possibility is our shared mission: My students are passionate about learning and I am passionate about teaching them. Or maybe it's the intimacy that develops between us. *Intimacy* isn't a term that usually comes to mind when describing student/teacher relationships. But that definitely describes the relationship I have had with some students, particularly those who only went to school for a few years or who never went to school at all. I imagine that for them, sitting in a classroom and being asked to participate in classroom-type activities is like being asked to bake a chocolate soufflé when you've only spent a few hours in a kitchen. By attending my class they unwittingly reveal to me all they *don't* know—how to answer a simple multiple choice question, how to address an envelope, where to write their name on a sign-in sheet. And that's what intimacy is all about, revealing a part of yourself that you normally keep hidden.

Feeling appreciated is another reward of teaching ESL. *Thank you for your patience* is what students often pen in notes they write to me during a lesson on letter writing. How could anyone not feel good about repeatedly being thanked simply for doing their job?

There is one final benefit of teaching ESL that's worth mentioning. I call it the "There but for the grace of God effect." This isn't something that kicks in at the end of my class but rather a feeling that sneaks up on me at odd moments. The last time it happened was when I was stuck in the Miami Airport for six hours trying to get home after my great uncle's one-hundredth birthday celebration. It was a "There but for the grace of God" moment because I started thinking about the fact that were it not for some very fortuitous circumstances that may or may not be attributable to God, I would never have been in that airport in the first place. Reading about social injustice didn't make me think this way. Watching PBS documentaries about people living in horrific conditions didn't do it either.

Rather, my ability to (sometimes) overlook life's frustrating yet inconsequential inconveniences comes from knowing about my students' lives and wondering how I ever got lucky enough to avoid the kinds of challenges they face every day.

I wouldn't be honest if I didn't admit that some days in the classroom are better than others. I also should add that I possess an odd confluence of attributes—interest in grammar, love of the Spanish language and Latin American culture, inability to teach other subjects to other types of students (I've tried and failed miserably), and an unrelenting need I've had since childhood to help the underdog—that makes me particularly well-suited for this job. That said, my initial sentiments hold: if you're fortunate enough to teach ESL to students who want to learn, you'll get at least as much out of it as they do.

The elephant in the room: Spanish in the classroom

A source of heated debate among ESL professionals is whether teachers should use the students' first language in the classroom. Traditionally adult ESL classes have been comprised of students from many countries, making it highly unlikely that a teacher would be able to speak the language of each of her students. An "English Only" policy on the part of the teacher is the only practical way to teach such classes. But the massive influx of immigrants from Latin America has resulted in an increased number of adult ESL classes, particularly beginning classes, which are comprised almost exclusively of Spanish speakers. Still, many academics continue to point to research that suggests that students will progress more rapidly when instructed exclusively in English.

I have not conducted any formal studies to support or negate this viewpoint. But I can speak from my own experience, which is that if all of your students, or even all of your students minus one or two, speak Spanish—and you also speak Spanish—your students will learn more if you view Spanish as one of many useful tools in your arsenal of teaching strategies. I find that this is particularly true if students haven't had a lot of formal education and therefore don't know the basics of grammar and sentence structure in their own language.

If you agree with the benefits of the teacher using some Spanish in the classroom, the obvious follow-on question is, "Exactly how much Spanish should I use?" I never had a satisfactory answer until one semester when I taught both an intermediate and low-beginning ESL class. I found that in my intermediate class, I used Spanish at most once or twice per class to translate particularly thorny vocabulary words. (*Disappointed* and *tin* are recent examples.) In my beginning class I used Spanish far more frequently, not only to translate new words but also to explain concepts and instructions that I was unable to communicate in English. Of course, as the semester progressed I used less and less Spanish, and I tried whenever possible, to act out, explain, or illustrate what I was saying. What that semester taught me was that once I got to know my students I instinctively knew how much Spanish to use based on how much English they understood.

What's important is the recognition that, as an ESL teacher, your job is to do whatever it takes to get your point across, which may mean using some Spanish.

Another role of a teacher, any teacher, is to listen to her students. When you are teaching beginning students, the only way to understand what they are saying is to speak their language. Thus, while you certainly don't need to know how to speak Spanish to teach a class of Spanish speakers, it is an asset.

Some ESL teachers with limited Spanish-speaking skills are hesitant about using it in the classroom. To me, that's a non-issue. The second language acquisition guru Stephen Krashen talks about the need for ESL teachers to "lower the affective filter," e.g. make the classroom a welcoming, anxiety-free environment where students feel comfortable making mistakes. There's no better way to do that than for students to see that their teacher's Spanish is almost as poor—or poorer—than their English.

How often students speak Spanish in the classroom is an entirely different question. If students are doing an exercise that requires speaking English, they certainly shouldn't be speaking Spanish. On the other hand, if you've just explained a new activity and students are conferring in Spanish about exactly what they need to do, speaking Spanish is appropriate since it's helping them achieve class objectives. The bottom line: students should speak only the Spanish they need to successfully complete their English assignments.

The role of grammar in adult ESL classes

Even though I write grammar books, I don't believe that grammar should be the focal point of ESL instruction. Communication should be the focal point of instruction, and gaining an understanding of basic grammar is one relatively small component of learning to communicate. That's why, for example, I recommend that, regardless of the length of your class, you not spend more than a quarter to a third of class time on the grammar exercises in *Paso a paso 1* and *Step by Step 1*. Doing worksheets is simply too passive an activity to be done for extended periods of time. Rather, devote the majority of class time to giving students opportunities to use English in speaking and listening activities that are relevant to their lives, be they activities in this book or other participatory activities you find appropriate.

Many ESL professionals are opposed to teaching grammar to beginning level students at all, believing that grammar is an obstruction that stands in the way of students' learning the rudiments of a new language. I have no doubt that this is true for children, who seem to miraculously learn second languages by osmosis. For adults my more than five years of classroom experience has taught me that the opposite is true. If adults learning a language are aware of the over-arching framework that defines the language, they are better able to use the vocabulary they have to express themselves in a variety of situations. I remember asking a student if she had a textbook. She thought for a moment, then carefully crafted her response, "Yes, I do". It doesn't seem like much, but for that student it was a huge accomplishment to be able to apply the grammar she had studied—which has no parallel structure in Spanish—to a real-life situation.

As a teacher you will need to sort out how central a role grammar will play in your overall curriculum. Keep in that you will invariably encounter students who for whatever reason are unable to make sense of even the most rudimentary grammar concepts. Many times these students have been in the United States for years and have figured out a way to communicate which though far from grammatically correct, gets the point across. My advice is to meet these students where they are by focusing your instruction for them almost exclusively on communicative (e.g. speaking and listening) activities.

When students stop coming

Teachers who teach English to adults rarely complain about their students. But if they do, it's almost always about the same thing: students' failure to come to class.

My first suggestion is not to take it personally. Many of the students you teach are most likely saddled with situations that conspire against their attending school—multiple jobs, lack of childcare, poor transportation options, limited access to medical care that translates into long waits at the clinic or, in many cases, no access to medical care at all.

That said, when students don't show you'll miss them in the same way you'd miss a dinner guest who doesn't show up at a big party you're hosting. (And most likely, you'll also be disappointed that they're not taking advantage of the great educational opportunity you're providing them!) One tactic is to get students' contact information on the first day of class and call them when they're absent. Chances are you're working with a population that is rarely lavished with attention, particularly by Americans, so your showing an interest in them means far more than you might expect. (If you don't speak Spanish, and your students don't speak much English, this is an ideal time to find a Spanish speaker to help you out.) Remember too that attending school in the U.S. as an immigrant adult is a far different experience than it is for a student who starts school here as a child—How many teachers have called you when you didn't show up for class?—but that's exactly my point. Our students are used to being invisible. In many cases, their illegal status forces them to be invisible. If you're going to keep them as students you may have to reach out to them in ways that teachers rarely turn to in more traditional teaching environments.

Recent research on *persistence* (the buzzword for the factors that contribute to students' staying in class) suggests that building a sense of community increases students' retention. But what exactly does *community* mean? That students know their classmates' names? That they have a friend to call if they have a question about class holidays? That they feel comfortable asking questions and making mistakes? It means all of those things. But to me, a community is also a place where people can be themselves and interact freely with one another. Fortunately, there's no better place to build such a community than in a language class. The premise behind this book is that students learning a language need to use that language by interacting with a variety of people in a variety of contexts. The very act of students getting out of their seats and speaking to their classmates about topics relevant to their everyday lives will do a great deal towards building a community which, theoretically, should make students more likely to continue coming to class.

Another factor discussed in research on persistence is goal setting. Not surprisingly, students who set goals, and feel that they're meeting those goals, are more motivated to continue coming to class. With a large class, goal setting is easier said than done. If can be difficult to decide on the focus of the class if, for example, you find that half your class's goal is to feel comfortable speaking to their child's teacher and the other half wants to speak enough English to find a job. Nonetheless, you should at a minimum ask your students, either informally or in a questionnaire, to identify their goals so you can keep them in mind as you develop lesson plans and create activities. If you're tutoring one or two students, or teaching a small class, it's far easier to focus on goal setting. You can ask students early on about their specific goals, then tailor the class to meet those needs and periodically check in with students to see how they perceive their progress.

Perception is everything

Learning a language as an adult is a slow, grueling, and often discouraging process. As a teacher, your goal is to keep your students interested, positive and, perhaps most important, confident in their ability to learn a new language. Stated another way, your goal is to make them feel like they're moving forward. I've already talked about the need for a balanced curriculum—too many grammar worksheets and students will have no clue how to use what they've learned; too much rote conversation and they won't know how to have a conversation without a script. But that's just a start. In addition to balancing the modalities you use to teach, you need to be mindful of the pace at which you teach it.

When I first started teaching ESL, I thought of learning a language as a linear process. You start with *a*, *an*, and *the*, move through the verb tenses, and voilà you're a fluent speaker. Of course, nothing could be farther from the truth. Learning a language is a messy endeavor, more like building a sand castle whose turrets get washed away, only to be rebuilt more sturdily the second, third, and fourth times around. In other words, students learn a language in fits and starts, often taking a step back before moving two steps ahead. Unless you're a tutor working with one or two students, you're never going to be able to ensure that all of your students understand, say, how to correctly use simple present tense verbs before you move on to the past tense. Your role as a teacher is to move at a pace that keeps fast learners engaged while still keeping slower learners in the game.

One way that this should *not* be done, no matter how tempting, is by asking students if they understand. Beginning students are very good at pretending to understand and it's not hard to see why. If you were learning a new language and someone asked you if you understood what was being said, it is far easier to nod your head in agreement than to admit your lack of understanding, only to have that person repeat the same incomprehensible explanation yet again. Thus, instead of asking students if they understand, you need to become an expert at asking them specific questions whose responses demonstrate their understanding. For example, if you're trying to explain the difference between *he* and *his*, ask students to give you a sentence that includes each one. If you're teaching the use of *has* and *have*, do the same thing. Constantly assessing your students, even if informally, will help you know when it's time to forge ahead.

I also recommend starting every class or tutoring session with a review. This is an instant reminder for students about what they've learned thus far. Given all there is to know about a language, students can feel daunted by everything they have to learn. One way to combat this is to remind them of how far they've come.

Another way to build students' sense of mastery is through quizzes. Many teachers don't like quizzes because they assume they put undue stress on students. But in reality the reverse is true. Giving students quizzes that they do well on builds confidence and increases their sense of accomplishment.

The well-stocked classroom

Yet another great aspect of teaching English is that you don't need a lot of stuff, though a few supplies can go a long way. Here are some useful additions to any language-learning environment. These materials also are called for throughout this book.

- Magazines (preferably ones with lots of pictures)
- Scissors (one per student or per two students)
- Individual white boards (class set. The boards should be roughly 12" by 18". You can get them at office supply stores or online.)
- Dry erase markers and socks/rags (class set; for use with the white boards)
- Scrap paper (This is essential if you don't have white boards.)
- Maps (of the US, your state, your city as well as the countries where your students are from)
- Dice (one for every two students)

About the activities in this book

My hope is that this book will help make your lesson planning a bit less time-consuming and will make your class a bit more enjoyable for your students. I know that the worksheets won't always be a perfect fit for your class. Rather you can view them as a springboard to use in developing ideas of your own. Ideally, you'll be able to personalize worksheets to include students' names, make them slightly easier or more difficult depending on your students' level, and so on. I'd love to hear about successful lessons you've developed, especially those that can be used in conjunction with *Paso a paso 1* and *Step by Step 1*. Send them to me at ElizabethWeal@tenaya.com. If I use them in future books, I'll be sure to give you credit.

Teacher's Diary

A Better Life

Whenever I despair over how difficult life in the U.S. is for my students, I think about how much harder it would be for them if they were living in their own country. Still, I occasionally have my doubts, especially when I read sentences like the ones below, written by intermediate-level students writing about what they used to do and what they didn't used to do in their country.

I used to feed horses.
I used to walk in the fields.
I used to fish in the river.
I used to swim in the river.
I used to eat my mother's cooking.
I used to run in the streets.
I used to drink agave water.
I used to eat iguana soup.
I used to see the sun rise on New Years day.

I didn't use to drive a car.
I didn't use to use a cell phone.
I didn't use to go shopping
I didn't use to see buildings
I didn't use to buy clothes.
I didn't use to spend a lot of time at home.
I didn't use to go to the gym.
I didn't use to work all the time.
I didn't use to eat pizza.

The Alphabet
(Class, Tutor/Tutee)

Objective
- Teach students the letters of the alphabet in English.

When to do this activity: During the first or second week of class.

Supplies
- *Alphabet* handout (with pronunciation in Spanish): one copy for each student
- White boards, dry erase markers and erasers (one for each student)

or

- 8 1/2" x 11" scrap paper cut in half (several sheets for each student)

How to introduce this activity
- Ask your students: *Why take the time to learn the alphabet in English?*

Activity: Part 1
- Distribute the alphabet handout.
- Repeat the alphabet. Explain that, on the handout, the pronunciation is in parentheses. (Many student won't realize this.)
- Teach *capital* (**mayúscula**) and *lower case* (**minúscula**).
- Write "problem letters" on the board and ask student to identify them. The most difficult letters are the vowels, *g, j, k, q, v, w, x, y,* and *z.*
- Almost all students have trouble distinguishing between *E* and *I.* Here's a tip you may want to pass on: Write a lower case E and put whiskers on it, then ask what people say when they see a mouse – *eeeee!* Write a lower case *I* and make the dot look like an eye.
- Pass out dry erase boards, markers, and erasers or large pieces of scrap paper.
- Call out a letter. Student must write the letter. Then hold it up for you to correct.
- Do this for capital and lower case letters.
- Repeat this activity in class for several days.

Activity: Part 2
- Dictate whole words to the students, especially long words, like *Mississippi* and *Wisconsin.* You might also try words like *exit, exercise, electrician, interviewer,* and *engineer* which force students to listen to distinguish between *e* and *i.*

Extension
- Display letters of the alphabet, uppercase and lowercase, around the room and practice them every day.

The Alphabet

A a	/ei/*
B b	/bi/
C c	/si/
D d	/di/
E e	/i/*
F f	/ef/
G g	/chi/
H h	/eich/
I i	/ai/*
J j	/che/
K k	/quei/
L l	/el/
M m	/em/
N n	/en/
O o	/ou/*
P p	/pi/
Q q	/quiu/
R r	/ar/
S s	/es/
T t	/ti/
U u	/iu/*
V v	/vi/
W w	/dabol iu/
X x	/exs/
Y y	/uai/
Z z	/tsi/

*Vowels: A, E, I, O, U

Consonants: all other letters (B, C, D, F, G, H, J, K, L, M, N, P, Q, R, S, T, V, W, X, Y, Z)

Using a Dictionary
(Class, Tutor/Tutee)

Objectives
- To teach students to use a simple dictionary. Many students won't know this!
- To encourage students to use the dictionary in the back of *Paso a paso* and *Step by Step* when they're completing exercises in the book.

When to do this activity: During the first or second week of class.

Supplies
- *Gramática del inglés: Paso a paso 1* or *English Grammar Step by Step 1*: one copy for each student
- *Dictionary Practice*: One for every two students

How to introduce this activity

Ask your students:

- *Why are dictionaries useful? (They tell you the meanings and pronunciations of words you don't know.)*
- *What skill do you need before you can use a dictionary? (You need to know the alphabet.)*

Activity: Part 1
- Ask students to turn to the dictionary on page 113 in their book. Then ask them to turn to the dictionary on page 117. Ask them to explain the difference. (e.g. *On page 113 the words are in English then Spanish and on page 117 they are in Spanish then English.)*
- Choose a letter from the Spanish/English dictionary, with relatively few words, say G. Ask students to explain why the words are ordered the way they are.
- Give students a word in English and ask them to tell you what page the word is on in the English/Spanish dictionary and what that word means in Spanish. Repeat this several times.
- Then give students a word in Spanish and ask them to tell you what page the word is on in the Spanish/English dictionary and what that word means in English. Repeat this several times.

Activity: Part 2
- Divide students into pairs.
- Give each pair a worksheet. Instruct them to use their Spanish/English and English/Spanish dictionaries in the back of their grammar book to answer the questions on the worksheet.
- When students finish, review the answers as a class.

📖 *Using a Dictionary*

Names

Translate these words from Spanish to English.

1 bajo   short

2 también

3 ojo

4 feo

5 suegro

6 pelota

7 guapo

8 padres

9 novio

10 limpio

Translate these words from English to Spanish.

1 garden   jardín

2 rice

3 tall

4 because

5 notebook

6 purple

7 toy

8 tree

9 girlfriend

10 niece

Extra credit. Using the English/Spanish dictionary find three English words that you don't know. Then, write what those words mean in Spanish.

English   **Spanish**

1

2

3

How do you say_____ in English?
(Class, Tutor/Tutee)

Objectives
- To teach students to use phonetic spellings to help in their pronunciation.
- To teach students the expression: **How do you say...**

When to do this activity: During the first or second week of class

Supplies
- *Gramática del inglés: Paso a paso 1* or *English Grammar Step by Step 1*: one copy for each student
- *How do you say.....in English?*: Class set

Teachers, take note: The phonetic spellings in the dictionary in the back of the grammar book are an attempt to make it as easy as possible for students to pronounce English words correctly. Sometimes this works well; for example, the long *e* sound in English translates nicely into a long *i* in Spanish. Other times, the translation is less clear cut. For example, there is no *th* sound in Spanish so we use *d*.

How to introduce this activity
- Discuss the lack of consistency in pronouncing words in English. (Words like **know** and **now**, **here** and **there**, and **laugh** and **ghost** are good examples.)
- Explain that phonetic spellings help students pronounce words in another language.
- Explain the use of the accent to show the syllable to emphasize:

    student (*stúdent*)   **orange** (*óransh*)   **divorced** (*divórst*)
- Emphasize that the phonetic spellings aren't foolproof. They're just a first step.

Activity 1
- Give each student a worksheet.
- Read the directions as a class.
- Ask students to complete the worksheet, that is, to find English words in their dictionary that they don't know and write those words on their worksheet, along with their meanings in Spanish.

Activity 2
- Write this conversation on the board:

    Student A: How do you say _____ in English?
    Student B: _____.
- Ask for two volunteers to come to the front of the class with their papers and practice this conversation using the new words they have learned. For example,

    Student A: How do you say *amigo* in English?
    Student B: *friend.*
- Students divide into pairs to practice the conversation.
- At the end of the class, students share some of the new words they have learned.

🙂🙂 *How do you say_____ in English?*

Name _____

Directions: Look in your English/Spanish dictionary. Write ten words you don't know in English. Try to pronounce each word. Then write what the word means in Spanish.

English words	Spanish translation
1.	
2.	
3.	
4.	
5.	
6.	
7.	
8.	
9.	
10.	

Objective

- To teach students to identify and spell the names of common items used in a classroom.

When to do this activity: During the first or second week of class

Supplies

- *Vocabulary: At school:* Class set
- Scissors for each student
- Paperclip for each student to clip their vocabulary cards

Before the class begins: Make sure you can identify each drawing: *book, notebook, pencil, pen, dictionary, pencil sharpener, table, chair whiteboard, marker, student, teacher.*

How to introduce this activity

- Ask students to identify various objects around the classroom (book, marker, whiteboard, etc.).

Activity: Part 1

- Distribute the worksheet *Vocabulary: At School.*
- Students cut out their cards.
- After students have cut out their cards, hold up a card and write what it is on the board. Students write the word in English <u>on the back</u> of the card.
- Do this for each card.

Activity: Part 2

- Divide students in pairs.
- Write this conversation on the board:

  > **Student A:** *What is this?*
  > **Student B:** *It is a _____.*
  > **Student A:** *Spell that please.* Please spell it
  > **Student B:** _____.

- Practice the conversation as a class.
- Students practice this conversation, showing their partner a vocabulary card; then asking their partner what it is and how to spell it.

Vocabulary: At school

Four Corners

(Class)

Objective
- Reinforce substituting pronouns for nouns.

When to do this activity: After students have completed Section 1.4 of *Paso a paso 1* or *Step by Step 1*.

Supplies
- *Four Corners cards.* (You need enough so that each student can have one card. If you need more, make your own.)

Before the class begins
- Cut out enough cards so that each student has one.
- On the white board, write **He**, **She**, and **They** in large letters evenly placed across the length of the board.
- If you don't have a white board, make three signs and post them around the room.

How to introduce this activity
- Write these nouns on the board:

     *Ana   Susan   The girls   Jose   Susan and An*a   *The boys   Jose and Ana*
- Ask students what subject pronoun they can substitute for each noun. Then write the pronoun under the noun.

Activity
- Give each student a card.
- Each student takes his card and stands under the appropriate sign (e.g. If your sign says **Ana** you stand under the **she** sign.)
- After students are standing under the appropriate sign, students take turns reading their cards. Other students give a *thumbs up* or *thumbs down* to indicate whether the student is standing in the correct location. If the student isn't in the correct location, they move.
- Collect cards and redistribute them, or do the activity again on another day.

Susan	The boy	Nina and Eduardo	My sister
Ana	The boys	The cooks	My friends
Maria and Leonardo	The students	The brothers	My friend
The girl	The teachers	Lucas, Ana, and Armondo	Armando
The girls	Anthony	My sisters	Deborah

Objectives
- Build fluency by providing an environment where students can easily converse with each other.
- Build a sense of community by helping students know the names and native countries of their classmates.
- Give students practice spelling their names.

When to do this activity: After students have completed Section 1.5 of *Paso a paso 1* or *Step by Step 1*.

Supplies
- *Classmate Interviews: Where are you from?* Class set

Teachers, take note: In Spanish, **nombre** means *first name*. That's why, when Spanish-speakers are asked their name, they often give only their first name. Explain that, in English, when people ask you your name, you usually give your first and last name unless it's a very informal situation.

How to introduce this activity
- Review the alphabet.
- Teach this vocabulary: *first name, last name, complete name.*

Activity
- Distribute a copy of *Classmate Interviews: Where are you from?* to each student.
- Display *Classmate Interviews: Where are you from?* so all students can see it or copy the conversation on the board.
- Read the conversation a line at a time; ask students to repeat each line as you read it.
- Ask for two student volunteers, one to ask the questions and one to answer them. The volunteers interview each other. Students who are seated record the results of these interviews on their interview forms. You may want to do this with a second pair of volunteers as well.
- Instruct students to move around the classroom, interviewing classmates so they can complete their forms.
- After everyone has completed their forms, ask students about their peers, e.g. *Where is Ana from? Where is Peter from?*
- Note: If most students are from the same country, change the question to *What city are you from?*

🙂🙂 Classmate Interviews: Where are you from?

Name _____

Student A: What is your first name?

Student B: My first name is _____

Student A: Spell that please.

Student B: _____

Student A: What is your last name?

Student B: My last name is _____

Student A: Spell that please.

Student B: _____

Student A: Where are you from?

Student B: I am from _____

First name	Last name	Country
1.		
2.		
3.		
4.		
5.		
6.		
7.		
8.		
9.		
10.		

U.S. Geography
(Class, Tutor/Tutee)

Objectives
- Learn the basics of US geography.
- Distinguish between *cities, states, and countries.*

When to do this activity: After students have completed Section 1.5 of *Paso a paso 1* or *Step by Step 1.*

Supplies
- Large map of North America (or, if you don't have one, use the same map you're giving to students)
- *U.S. map:* class set
- *US Geography 1* handout: one for every pair of students
- *US Geography 1* handout: one for every pair of students

How to introduce this activity
- Using a map of North America, demonstrate the difference between *city, state, and country.*

Activity 1
- Give every student a map of North America.
- Ask students questions about the map (e.g. *Is Oregon a city or a state?*)
- Give every pair of students a *US Geography* worksheet.
- Students work in pairs to answer the questions on the worksheet. They don't need to write complete sentences.
- Review the answers as a class.

Activity 2
- Repeat Activity 1 the following day using the *Geography 2* handout.

 # U.S. Geography 1

Names_____

Directions: Use your map to answer each question. You don't need to write a complete sentence.

1. Is Texas a city or state? _____

2. Is Florida a city or state? _____

3. Is Mexico a state or a country? _____

4. Is Canada a state or a country? _____

5. Is California a city or a state? _____

6. Is Los Angeles in Oregon? _____

7. Is Las Vegas in Nevada? _____

8. Is Salt Lake City in Utah? _____

9. Is Miami in Florida? _____

10. Is Dallas a city or a state? _____

11. Is the United States a state or a country? _____

12. Write five cities in the United States.

_____   _____   _____

_____   _____

13. Write five states in the United States.

_____   _____   _____

_____   _____

14. Write three countries in North America.

_____   _____   _____

15. What city are you in now? _____

16. What state are you in now? _____

 # U.S. Geography 2

Names_____

Directions: Use your map to answer each question. You don't need to write a complete sentence.

1. Is California a city or state? _____

2. Is Los Angeles a city or state? _____

3. Is Mexico a state or a country? _____

4. Is Canada a state or a country? _____

5. Is Houston a city or a state? _____

6. Is Houston in California? _____

7. Is Seattle in Washington? _____

8. Is Salt Lake City in Texas? _____

9. Is Las Vegas in Nevada? _____

10. Is Nevada a city or a state? _____

11. Is the United States a state or a country? _____

12. What city do you live in? _____

13. What country do you live in? _____

14. What state do you live in? _____

U.S. Map

Objectives

- Build fluency by providing an environment where students can easily converse with each other.
- Reinforce the difference between *city* and *country*.
- Build a sense of community by helping students know the names and native countries of their classmates.

When to do this activity: After students have completed Section 1.5 of *Paso a paso 1* or *Step by Step 1*.

Supplies

- *Classmate Interviews: What city are you from?* Class set

Teachers, take note: Many of your students probably will be from small towns. Thus, you may want to explains that ***city*** is sometimes used to refer to small towns as well as large metropolises.

How to introduce this activity

- Review the alphabet.
- Review this vocabulary: *first name, last name, complete name, city, country.*

Activity

- Distribute a copy of *Classmate Interviews: What city are you from?* to each student.
- Display a copy so everyone can see it or copy the conversation on the board.
- Read the conversation, with students repeating each line after you read it.
- Note that *name* can refer to either *first name* or *complete name.* In this exercise students should use their complete names.
- Ask for two student volunteers, one to ask the questions and one to answer them. The volunteers interview each other. Students who are seated record the results of these interviews on their interview forms.
- Students move around the class interviewing fellow students and completing their forms.
- After everyone has completed their interviews, ask students about their peers, e.g. *What city is Ana from? What country is Ana from?*

Classmate Interviews: What city are you from?

Name _____

Student A: What is your name?

Student B: My name is _____

Student A: Spell that please.

Student B: _____

Student A: What city are you from?

Student B: I am from _____

Student A: What country are you from?

Student B: I am from _____

Name	City	Country
1.		
2.		
3.		
4.		
5.		
6.		
7.		
8.		
9.		
10.		

Completing a Student Information Form
(Class, Tutor/Tutee)

Objectives
- Practice completing simple forms.
- Practice using the alphabet to dictate personal information.

When to do this activity: After students have completed Section 1.5 of *Paso a paso 1* or *Step by Step 1*.

Supplies
- *Completing a Student information form:* Class set

Teachers, take note:
- Make sure to explicitly teach students where the spaces and dashes go when writing a phone number. Many Latin American countries have different conventions when writing phone numbers which students naturally want to use when they write their phone number in the US.
- This activity focuses on such a critical skill that you may want to repeat it more than once, with students interviewing different students each time.

How to introduce this activity
- Introduce this vocabulary: *middle initial, street address, zip code, area code, phone number, birthplace.*
- Review this vocabulary: *first name, last name, city, state.*

Activity 1
- Pass out *Completing A Student Information Form* worksheet.
- Student complete the first form for themselves.

Activity 2
- Write these questions on the board:
    What is your last name?
    What is your first name?
    What is your middle initial?
    What is your street address?
    What is your city?
    What is your state?
    What is your telephone number?
    What is your birthplace?
- Display the worksheet, *Completing a Studental Information Form.* Point to a line on the form and ask students to tell you what question they need to ask to elicit the necessary information.
- Students interview two students and complete the form for them. Of course, each student will also be interviewed twice.

✍ *Completing a Student Information Form*

Directions: Complete this form for yourself.

Last name _____ First name _____ Middle initial ___

Street address _____

City_____ State _____ Zip code _____

Telephone number _____

Birthplace _____

Directions: Complete this form for a classmate.

Last name _____ First name _____ Middle initial ___

Street address _____

City_____ State _____ Zip code _____

Telephone number _____

Birthplace _____

Directions: Complete this form for a classmate.

Last name _____ First name _____ Middle initial ___

Street address _____

City_____ State _____ Zip code _____

Telephone number _____

Birthplace _____

Conversation Practice
(Class, Tutor/Tutee)

Objective
- Build fluency by providing an environment where students repeat the same conversation multiple times and therefore gain fluency.

When to do this activity: After students have completed Chapter 1 of *Paso a paso 1* or *Step by Step 1*.

Supplies
- Class set of the *Conversation Practice* you're doing that day.

How to introduce this activity
- Introduce new vocabulary used in the conversation for that day.
- If you are doing a conversation that includes a question with many possible responses, such as *What is your favorite sport?* make a list of possible responses on the board.

Activity
- Pass out the *Conversation Practice* worksheet and practice the conversation as a class, focusing on pronunciation.
- Students stand in two lines facing each other, line 1 and line 2.
- Student A interviews the student he's facing, Student B. Then, Student B interviews Student A. When students have completed their conversations, you instruct them to change partners:
  - Students in line 1 move to the right. The student at the end of the line moves to the beginning of the line.
  - Students in line 2 don't move.
- The result: Everyone has a new partner and they practice the interview again.

Challenge
- After students have practiced the conversation with several different partners, ask them to practice the conversation without looking at their papers.
- At the end of the activity, ask pairs of students to practice the conversation in front of the class without using their papers.

Conversation Practice

Conversation Practice 1.1: Introductions

Student A: Hi.

Student B: Hi.

Student A: What is your name?

Student B: My name is _____ What is your name?

Student A: My name is _____.

Student B: Nice to meet you.

Student A: Nice to meet you, too.

Conversation Practice 1.2: Where are you from?

Student A: Hello.

Student B: Hi.

Student A: What is your name?

Student B: My name is _____.

Student A: Where are you from?

Student B: _____.

Student A: Nice to meet you.

Student B: Nice to meet you, too.

👥 *Conversation Practice*

Conversation Practice 1.3: Student information

Student A: What is your name?

Student B: My name is _____

Student A: How are you today?

Student B:

   I'm terrific.

   I'm fine.

   I'm ok.

   I'm not so good.

Student A: I want to send you some information. What is your address?

Student B: My address is _____

Student A: What is your telephone number?

Student B: My telephone number is _____

Student A: Where are you from?

Student B: _____

Student A: Nice to talk to you.

Student B: Nice to talk to you, too.

 # Conversation Practice

Conversation Practice 1.4: Favorites

Student A: Hi.

Student B: Hi.

Student A: What is your name?

Student B: My name is _____

Student A: What is your favorite color?

Student B: My favorite color is _____

Student A: What is your favorite sport?

Student B: My favorite sport is _____

Student A: Thanks for your time.

Student B: You're welcome.

Conversation Practice 1.5: More Favorites

Student A: Hi.

Student B: _____

Student A: What is your name?

Student B: My name is _____

Student A: What is your favorite kind of ice cream?

Student B: My favorite kind of ice cream is _____

Student A: What is your favorite kind of pizza?

Student B: My favorite kind of pizza is _____

Student A: What is your favorite kind of music?

Student B: My favorite kind of music is _____

Student A: Thanks for your time.

Student B: You're welcome.

Scrambled Sentences
(Class, Tutor/Tutee)

Objectives
- Reinforce the notion that sentences are comprised of words that can be combined in many different ways.
- Reinforce the use of the verb *to be*.

When to do this activity: After students have completed Chapter 1 of *Paso a paso 1* or *Step by Step 1*.

Supplies
- *Scrambled Sentences Word Cards:* one for every two students
- *Scrambled Sentences Record Sheet* one for every two students
- Scissors for every two students

How to introduce this activity
- Review how to conjugate the verb *to be*.

Activity
- Divide students in pairs. (Try to match students of similar ability levels. Less advanced students may only write five or six sentences while more advanced students can aim to complete their record sheets and then write more sentences on the back.)
- Give each pair a set of *Scrambled Sentence Word Cards*, a record sheet, and a pair of scissors.
- Students cut out the word cards.
- Working in pairs, students make as many sentences as they can using only the words on the card. Students record each sentence on the record sheet.
- There are more than 25 possible sentences.
- As students finish, ask them to write one or two sentences on the board.

Scrambled Sentences Word Cards

Susan	The boy	Pedro and Pablo	My sister
They	I	She	He
You	the United States	Mexico	Honduras
am	is	are	from

Scrambled Sentences Record Sheet

Names _____

1 _____

2 _____

3 _____

4 _____

5 _____

6 _____

7 _____

8 _____

9 _____

10 _____

11 _____

12 _____

13 _____

14 _____

15 _____

16 _____

17 _____

18 _____

19 _____

20 _____

Teacher's Diary

My Daily Routine
(From a student's essay)

I get up at 3:30. I brush my teeth. I comb my hair. I go to work. I start at 4:00. I vacuum. I take out the trash. I dust. I sweep the floor. I mop the floor. I clean the windows. I finish work at 9 a.m. And after work, I go to school at Sequoia Adult School. I go from 9 to 12 and after school I go home. I eat lunch at about 12:30. I go to bed at 1:00. I get up at 4:00. I go to work. I start at 5:00 p.m. I drive to work. I vacuum. I dust. I take out the trash. I work five hours. My wife and my son help me at work. We return at 10:00. I eat dinner at 11:00. I go to sleep. I get up at 3:30…

Vocabulary: *Jobs*
(Class, Tutor/Tutee)

Objective
- To teach students to identify and spell the names of common jobs, including their own job.

When to do this activity: After students have completed Section 2.2 of *Paso a paso 1* or *Step by Step 1*.

Supplies
- *Vocabulary: Jobs:* Class set
- Scissors for each student
- Paperclip for each student to clip their vocabulary cards

Before the class begins: Make sure you can identify each job: *painter, cashier, construction worker, cook, homemaker, engineer, gardener/landscaper, house cleaner, nurse, babysitter, salesperson, waiter.*

How to introduce this activity
- Ask a few students, *What is your job?*

Activity: Part 1
- Distribute *Vocabulary: Jobs.*
- Students cut out their cards.
- After students have cut out their cards, hold up a card and write the name of the job on the board. Students write the word in English <u>on the back</u> of the card.
- Do this for each card.

Activity: Part 2
- Divide students in pairs.
- Write this conversation on the board:

> **Student A:** *What is his job?*
> **Student B:** *He is a* _____.
> **Student A:** *Spell that please.*
> **Student B:** _____
> **Student A:** *What is her job?*
> **Student B:** *She is a* _____.
> **Student A:** *Spell that please.*
> **Student B:** _____

- Explain that *his* is the possessive pronoun for males and *her* is the possessive pronoun for females.
- Practice the conversation as a class, with you holding up the pictures and students identifying who it is.
- Ask a pair of students to demonstrate the conversation.
- Students practice this conversation in pairs, with one student showing their partner a vocabulary card; then practicing the dialogue.

Objectives
- Build fluency by providing an environment where students can easily converse with each other.
- Teach students the names of common jobs.
- Give students practice spelling their names.

When to do this activity: After students have completed Section 2.2 of *Paso a paso 1* or *Step by Step 1*.

Supplies
- *Classmate Interviews: What is your job?* Class set

Teachers, take note: Many students will omit the article when talking about their job. That's because, in Spanish, you say, for example, *Soy maestra*, which literally means, *I am teacher.*

How to introduce this activity
- Ask each student, *What is your job?*
- Make a list of their responses on the board.
- If a student doesn't have a job they can reply, *I am a student* or *I am a homemaker* or *I am unemployed.*
- Ask students about their classmates' jobs, e.g. *What is Alma's job?*

Activity
- Distribute a copy of *Classmate Interviews: What is your job?* to each student.
- Display *Classmate Interviews: What is your job?* so all students can see it or write the conversation on the board.
- Practice the conversation as a class.
- Ask for two student volunteers, one to ask the questions and one to answer them. The volunteers interview each other. Students who are seated record the results of these interviews on their interview forms.
- Instruct students to move around the classroom, interviewing classmates so they can complete their forms.
- After everyone has completed their forms, ask students about their peers, e.g. *What is Nester's job; What is Laura's job?* This will give students more practice using personal pronouns.

Extension: Repeat this exercise but tell students they can pretend to have any job they'd like. In other words, change the worksheet question from *What is your job?* to *What is your dream job?* Students write the job they'd like to have rather than the jobs they have. You're bound to get some interesting responses: *mayor, truant officer, singer,* etc.

🙂🙂 Classmate Interviews: What is your job?

Name _____

Student A: What is your first name?

Student B: My first name is _____

Student A: Spell that please.

Student B: _____

Student A: What is your job?

Student B: I am a_____

Student A: Nice to talk to you.

Student B: Nice to talk to you too.

First name	Job
1.	
2.	
3.	
4.	
5.	
6.	
7.	
8.	
9.	
10.	

Vocabulary: *Adjectives*
(Class, Tutor/Tutee)

Objective
- To teach students to identify and spell the names of common adjectives

When to do this activity: After students have completed Section 2.4 of *Paso a paso 1* or *Step by Step 1*.

Supplies
- *Vocabulary: Adjectives:* Class set
- Scissors for each student
- Paperclip for each student to clip their *Adjectives* vocabulary cards

How to introduce this activity
- Review the definition of an *adjective* (*a word that describes a noun or pronoun*).
- Write several words on the board (e.g. *book, happy, tired, is, tall*) and have students tell you which words are adjectives.

Activity 1
- Distribute *Vocabulary: Adjectives:*
- Students cut out Adjective Cards.
- Ask students to write the translation of the adjective on the back of the card. (They should have learned these words by completing Section 2.4 of *Paso a paso 1* or *Step by Step 1*.)
- Review translations to make sure they're correct.

Activity 2
- Introduce *opposite* and ask students for some examples of words that are opposites.
- Divide students into pairs.
- One student takes out his/her Adjective Cards. The other student puts his cards away.
- When you say *go* Students must pair each card with its opposite. The first pair of students that correctly matches all their cards is the winner.

Activity 3
- Divide students into pairs.
- Write these sentences on the board:
    Student A: *What is the opposite of _____?*
    Student B: *The opposite of _____ is _____*
- Students quiz each other by showing their partner a card, then asking their partner what its opposite is.

Extension:
- You also can ask students to stand in two lines, and practice quizzing each other this way. See Exercise 2d for an explanation of how to do this.

Vocabulary: Adjectives

tall	beautiful/pretty	hardworking	healthy
short	ugly	lazy	sick
thin	happy	good	young
heavy	sad	bad	old

Conversation Practice: Describing people
(Class, Tutor/Tutee)

Objectives
- Build fluency by using adjectives in conversation.
- Reinforce adjectives vocabulary.

When to do this activity: After students have have completedd Section 2.4 of *Paso a paso 1* or *Step by Step 1*.

Supplies
- *Describing People:* Class set

Before the class begins
- On the board, write a list of adjectives that can be used to describe people. Use adjectives in Chapter 2 of *Paso a Paso* and add a few of your own (***serious, quiet, funny, calm, nervous,*** etc.).

How to introduce this activity
- Introduce new vocabulary: ***describe, best friend, yourself***.
- Review the definition of *adjective*.
- Talk about the adjectives you have written on the board.
- Display a copy of *Conversation Practice: Describing People* or write the conversation on the board. (Don't give students a copy or they'll write down their answers!)
- As a class, practice asking the questions, working on pronunciation.
- Explain how to say *I don't have a* _____ in case the student doesn't have a sister, brother, best friend, etc.
- Ask for volunteers to ask and answer the questions. Make sure that all answers are complete sentences.

Activity
- Distribute *Conversation Practice: Describing People.*
- Students stand in two lines facing each other, line 1 and line 2.
- Student A interviews the student he's facing, Student B. Then, Student B interviews Student A.
- When students have completed their conversations, you instruct them to change partners:
    - Students in line 1 move to the right. The student at the end of the line moves to the beginning of the line.
    - Students in line 2 don't move.
- The result: Everyone has a new partner and they practice the interview again.

Challenge
Ask students to practice their conversation without looking at their papers.

Conversation Practice: Describing people

Student A: Describe your sister.

Student B: My sister is _____, _____ and _____.

Student A: Describe your brother.

Student B: My brother is _____, _____ and

_____.

Student A: Describe your best friend.

Student B: My best friend is _____, _____ *and*

_____.

Student A: Describe yourself.

Student B: I am _____, _____ and _____.

Listening Practice: Famous People
(Class, Tutor/Tutee)

Objectives
- Improve listening comprehension.
- Build confidence in students' ability to write what they hear.

When to do this activity: After students have completed Section 2.4 of *Paso a paso 1* or *Step by Step 1.*

Supplies
- *Listening Practice: Famous People:* class set

Before the class begins
- Before class starts, privately interview five students. Ask them the city and country they're from, their job, and their favorite sport or hobby. You'll use this information in the listening practice.

How to introduce this activity
- Introduce new vocabulary: **hobby** (*pasatiempo*).
- Go around the room, asking students their favorite sport or hobby. Make a list of their responses on the board.

Activity
- Pass out the *Listening Practice: Famous People* worksheet.
- Read the instructions on the worksheet.
- Read each of the descriptions below. After completing each one, stop to give students time to write the correct information on their worksheet. Encourage students to ask you to spell words they don't know by saying *Spell that please.* You'll also need to explain new vocabulary like *retired* and *dancer.* Read each paragraph as many times as necessary.

    Barak Obama is from Honolulu, a city in the United States. He is President of the United States. His favorite sport is basketball.

    Hugo Sanchez is from Mexico City, Mexico. He was a famous soccer player. Now he is retired. His favorite sport is soccer.

    Salma Hayek is from Coatzacoalcos, Mexico. She is an actress. Her favorite hobby is dancing.

- Read the paragraphs that describe students in your class and have students complete their forms accordingly. Or make up your own paragraphs about famous people.
- Review the answers as a class.

🔊 *Listening Practice: Famous People*

Name _____

Directions: Listen to your teacher. Then complete the chart.

Name	City	Country	Job	Favorite sport or hobby
1. Barak Obama				
2. Hugo Sanchez				
3. Salma Hayak				
4.				
5.				
6.				
7.				
8.				

Objectives
- Reinforce the names of colors.
- Reinforce the distinction between *this* and *these*.
- Reinforce when to use *it* and when to use *they*.

When to do this activity: After students have completed Section 2.8 of *Paso a paso 1* or *Step by Step 1*.

Supplies
- A pack of construction paper with as many of these colors as possible: *red, yellow, green, blue, orange, purple, brown, black, white, gray.*
- *Conversation Practice: Talking about Colors*: class set

How to introduce this activity
- Review the colors.
- Point to objects in the classroom and ask, *What color is this?* and *What color are these?*

Activity 1
- Give each student four pieces of paper, two of one color and two of another.
- Distribute the *Talking About Colors* worksheet.
- Practice Conversation 1 as a class, focusing on pronunciation.
- Demonstrate the activity with two volunteers who come to the front of the class and demonstrate the conversation. (Remind students to show their paper to their partner when they ask their partner to identify the color of the paper.)
- Students stand in two lines facing each other, line 1 and line 2.
- Student A interviews the student he's facing, Student B. Then, Student B interviews Student A.
- When students have completed their conversations, you instruct them to change partners:
  - Students in line 1 move to the right. The student at the end of the line moves to the beginning of the line.
  - Students in line 2 don't move.
- The result: Everyone has a new partner and they practice the interview again.

Activity 2
- Review vocabulary used in Conversation 2: *hair, eyes, shoes, shirt.*
- Repeat the above procedure for Conversation 2.

👥 Conversation Practice: *Talking about colors*

Conversation 1

Student A: What color is this?

Student B: It is _____

Student A: What color are these?

Student B: *They are* _____ and _____

Conversation 2

Student A: What color is your hair?

Student B: It is _____

Student A: What color are your eyes?

Student B: They are _____.

Student A: *What color are your shoes?*

Student B: They are _____

Student A: What color is your shirt?

Student B: It is _____

Four Corners

(Class)

Objective
- Reinforce substituting pronouns for nouns.

When to do this activity: After students have completed Section 2.9 of *Paso a paso 1* or *Step by Step 1*.

Supplies
- *Four Corners cards.* (You need enough so that each student can have one card. If you need more, make your own.)

Before the class begins
- Cut out enough cards so that each student can have one card.
- On the white board, write **He**, **She**, **It**, **We**, and **They** in large letters, evenly spaced across the length of the board.
- If you don't have a white board, make signs and post them around the room.

How to introduce this activity
- Write these nouns on the board:

       Luis   Angelica   The students   the book   the books   Jesus and I

Ask students what subject pronoun they can substitute for each one.

Activity
- Give each student a card.
- Each student takes his card and stands under the appropriate sign (e.g. If your sign says *the book* you stand under the *it* sign.)
- After students are standing under the appropriate sign, students take turns reading their cards. Other students give a *thumbs up* or *thumbs down* to indicate whether the student is standing in the correct location. If the student isn't in the correct location, they move.

Laura	My dog	Pablo	My father
Gerardo	The computer	The doctors	My sister and I
Lillian	The cars	The cooks	My brother
Lucas	The computers	The cook	My sisters
The car	The teacher and I	Lucas, Ana, and Armonda	My house

Adjectives Scavenger Hunt
(Class, Tutor/Tutee)

Objectives
- Encourage students to use their knowledge of adjectives in new ways.
- Reinforce adjectives vocabulary.

When to do this activity: After students have completed Chapter 2 of *Paso a paso 1* or *Step by Step 1*.

Supplies
- *Adjectives Scavenger Hunt*: Class set
- Old magazines with lots of pictures
- Scissors (one for every two or three students)
- Tape or glue stick (one for every two or three students)

Before the class begins
- Cut out four pictures of individuals from a magazine. Tape or glue each picture onto a square in the *Adjectives Scavenger Hunt* worksheet.

How to introduce this activity
- On the whiteboard, brainstorm adjectives that can be used to describe people. Divide these adjectives into two groups:
    - Physical characteristics (e.g. *tall, short, heavy, thin, pretty, beautiful, handsome, ugly, young, old*)
    - Other characteristics (*happy, sad, tired, excited, nervous, serious, funny, lazy, hardworking*)
- Display the pictures you have cut out and ask students to give you adjectives from the list on the board to describe each picture.
- Under each picture, write a sentence that describes the student, e.g. *He is young, tall, and handsome.*
- Explain where the commas go and remind students to start each sentence with a capital letter and end it with a period.

Activity
- Distribute supplies.
- Ask for a volunteer to read the directions on their worksheet. Discuss directions.
- Students complete the assignment, then share with classmates.

✍️ *Adjectives Scavenger Hunt*

Name _____

Directions: Cut out a picture of a person. Attach it to your paper. Then write a sentence that includes at least three adjectives that describe that person.

Scrambled Sentences
(Class, Tutor/Tutee)

Objectives
- Reinforce the idea that sentences are comprised of words that can be combined in many different ways.
- Reinforce the use of sentences that include adjectives and the verb *to be*.

When to do this activity: After students have completed Chapter 2 of *Paso a paso 1* or *Step by Step 1*.

Supplies
- *Scrambled Sentences Word Cards:* one for every two students
- *Scrambled Sentences Record Sheet* one for every two students
- Scissors for every two students

How to introduce this activity
- Review how to conjugate the verb *to be*.
- Introduce new vocabulary words: ***serious*** and ***funny.***

Activity
- Divide students in pairs. (Try to match students of similar ability levels. Less advanced students may only write five or six sentences while more advanced students can aim to complete their record sheets and then write more sentences on the back.)
- Give each pair a set of word cards, a record sheet, and a pair of scissors.
- Students cut out the word cards.
- Working in pairs, students make as many sentences as they can using only the words on their cards. Students record each sentence on the record sheet.
- There are more than 25 possible sentences.
- As students finish, ask them to write one or two sentences on the board.
- Review sentences as a class.

They	I	He	Luis
You	is	She	are
lazy	We	am	serious
and	hardworking	funny	Laura

Scrambled Sentences Record Sheet

Names

1 _____

2 _____

3 _____

4 _____

5 _____

6 _____

7 _____

8 _____

9 _____

10 _____

11 _____

12 _____

13 _____

14 _____

15 _____

16 _____

17 _____

18 _____

19 _____

20 _____

Teacher's Diary

Where not to sell Spanish grammar books

Soon after writing my grammar books, it occurred to me that I needed to devote some time to selling them. And to sell books, especially to schools, it helps to have sales reps. I first published my books a few years ago, before Arizona had passed its notorious anti-immigration laws, so I thought nothing of calling a sales rep from Arizona to try to drum up a little business.

After introducing myself, and giving my usual spiel about how most grammar books on the market for ESL students are too advanced for students who don't know much about grammar in their own language, I told the rep the name of my book, Gramática del inglés: Paso a paso.

"Not good," she said. "We can only sell books in English."

"But there's an English version," I said cheerfully. "It's called English Grammar: Step by Step."

"That sounds just like what we need," she said. "ESL students here have grammar for an hour every day. And they need something simple that moves slowly."

"Great," I said. "But I should tell you that there are a few Spanish words even in the English version. For example, there's a Spanish/English dictionary at the back of the book.

"That won't work," she told me. "We can't use books that have a word of Spanish in them."

"So you couldn't use the English version of the book with your Spanish speakers?" I persisted.

"Well, it sounds like it would be perfect for the Spanish speakers except that it can't have a word of Spanish in it."

We ended the conversation there.

Vocabulary: *Contractions*
(Class, Tutor/Tutee)

Objective
- Reinforce the idea that a contraction (e.g. *He's*) and its non-contraction form (e.g. *He is*) mean the same thing.

When to do this activity: After students have completed Section 3.1 of *Paso a paso 1* or *Step by Step 1*.

Supplies
- *Vocabulary: Contractions:* Class set
- Scissors for each student
- Paperclip for each student to clip their vocabulary cards

Teachers, take note: Students often have a difficult time understanding contractions since they don't realize that they are just a shortened form of the same construction. (e.g. They don't necessarily understand that *I am* means the same thing as *I'm*.) Thus, it is important to repeat this point on multiple occasions.

How to introduce this activity
- Review contractions with the verb *to be* (*I'm, you're, he's, she's, it's, we're, they're*).
- Practice pronouncing each contraction.

Activity: Part 1
- Distribute *Contraction Vocabulary* Cards.
- Students cut out their *Contraction Vocabulary* Cards.
- Ask students to write the correct contraction on the back of the card.
- Review cards as a class to make sure students have written the correct contraction on the back of the card.

Activity: Part 2
- Write this conversation on the board:

    Student A: *What is the contraction for* _____ _____?
    Student B: *The contraction for* _____ _____*is* _____
- Practice the conversation.
- Demonstrate this activity with two volunteers who come to the front of the class with their Contraction Cards.
    - Student 1 holds up one of his cards and asks Student 2
      *What is the contraction for **you are**?*
    - Without looking at his card, Student 2 replies
      *The contraction for **you are** is _____*
- Students form two lines facing each other and quiz each other on the contractions. After a few minutes, they change partners. (See Section 2.d for more detailed instructions on how to do this.)

I am	you are	he is	she is
it is	we are	they are	

From Negative to Affirmative

(Class, Tutor/Tutee)

Objective
- Gain fluency using affirmative and negative sentences with the verb *to be*.

When to do this activity: After students complete Section 3.2 of *Paso a paso 1* or *Step by Step 1*.

Supplies
- One copy *From Negative to Affirmative*

Before you begin the class: Cut out sentence strips on the *From Negative to Affirmative* worksheet. You'll need one for each student.

How to introduce this activity
- Review the definition of *affirmative* and *negative*.
- Ask students to give you examples of each.

Activity
- Students stand in a line in front of the class.
- Distribute a sentence strip to each student.
- Each student reads the negative form of their sentence, adding an appropriate affirmative sentence. For example,

    I am not from the United States. I am from Mexico.
- After each students has a turn, collect and redistribute sentence strips.

Extension
- Make up your own sentence strips using students in your class. For example,

    Maria is from Japan.
    Andres is at home now.

👥 From Negative to Affiirmative

I am from the United States.
I am a teacher.
I am at home.
I am from Canada.
I am 12 years old.
I am at a party.
Right now, I am in Guadalajara.
I am sick today.
The students are lazy.
The sky is red.
The sun is pink.
Barak Obama is an engineer.
Miami is a state.
Florida is a city.
Today is Saturday.
Salma Hayek is from El Salvador.
Shakira is from Mexico.
Vicente Fernández is from the United States.
California is a country.
The United States is a small country.
Leonardo DeCaprio is from Russia.
Apples are white.
Grapes are black.
Jennifer Lopez is from China.
The year is 2009.

Vocabulary: *Negative Contractions*
(Class, Tutor/Tutee)

Objective
- Reinforce the idea that a negative contraction (e.g *He isn't*) and its non-contraction form (e.g. *He is not*) mean the same thing.

When to do this activity: After students complete Section 3.3 of *Paso a paso 1* or *Step by Step 1.*

Supplies
- *Vocabulary: Negative Contractions:* Class set
- Scissors for each student
- Paperclip for each student to clip their vocabulary cards

Teachers take note: In English, there are two ways of forming negative contractions with the verb *to be* for all contractions other than *I'm not.* For example, you can say *you aren't* or you can say *you're not.* To keep things simple, *Paso a paso 1* and *Step by Step 1* only teach the first form (*you aren't*). Appendix B of *Paso a Paso 1* and *Step by Step 1* explains the second form; send students to that appendix if they ask want to learn about both ways to form contractions.

How to introduce this activity
- Review negative contractions with the verb *to be* (*I'm, you aren't, he isn't, she isn't we aren't, they aren't*).
- Practice pronouncing each contraction.

Activity 1
- Distribute *Negative Contraction Vocabulary Cards.*
- Students cut out their *Contraction Vocabulary Cards.*
- Ask students to write the correct contraction on the back of the card.
- Review the negative contractions to make sure students have written the correct contraction on the back of the card.

Activity 2
- Write this conversation on the board:
   > ***Student A:*** *What is the contraction for* _____ _____ _____?
   > ***Student B:*** *The contraction for* _____ _____ _____ *is* _____ _____
- Practice the conversation as a class. _____
- Demonstrate this activity with two volunteers who come to the front of the class with their Contraction Cards.
   - Student 1 holds up one of his cards and asks Student 2
      *What is the contraction for **you are not?***
   - Without looking at his card, Student 2 replies
      *The contraction for **you are not** is* _____
- Students form two lines facing each other and quiz each other on the contractions. After a few minutes, they change partners. (See Section 2.d for more detailed instructions on how to do this.)

📚 *Vocabulary: Negative Contractions*

I am not	you are not	he is not	she is not
it is not	we are not	they are not	

Contractions Dictation
(Class, Tutor/Tutee)

Objectives
- Reinforce the difference in pronunciation between sentences that include contractions and those that don't.
- Understand sentences with and without contractions.
- Practice writing sentences with and without contractions.

When to do this activity: After students have completed Section 3.4 of *Paso a paso 1* or *Step by Step 1*.

Supplies
- A piece of paper for each student

How to introduce this activity
- Review affirmative and negative contractions, focusing on pronunciation.

Activity
- Give each student a piece of paper.
- Dictate the following sentences to your students, or make up your own. Repeat each sentence twice. Then, after you've read all of the sentences, ask students if they need you to repeat any sentences. (You'll probably want to do one list each day for several days.)

List 1: Some sentences include affirmative contractions	List 2: Some sentences include negative contractions	List 3: Some sentences include affirmative or negative contractions
1. I am tired.	1. I am not from Mexico.	1. We are not sad.
2. I'm tired.	2. I'm not from Mexico.	2. We aren't sad.
3. She's a teacher.	3. He isn't a student.	3. We're sad.
4. She is a teacher.	4. He is not a student.	4. They aren't lazy.
5. You are my friend.	5. You are not late.	5. They are not lazy.
6. You're my friend.	6. You aren't late.	6. They're lazy.
7. It's hot today.	7. Ana is not my sister.	7. My books are here.
8. It is hot today.	8. Ana isn't my sister.	8. My books are not here.
9. We're from Mexico.	9. It isn't cold today.	9. My books aren't here.
10. We are from Mexico.	10. It is not cold today.	10. I'm late.

- Ask different students to come to the board to write the sentences. Students correct their own papers.

Tell the Truth
(Class, Tutor/tutee)

Objectives
- Practice affirmative and negative statements.
- Practice *this* vs. *that*.

When to do this activity: After students have completed Section 3.4 of *Paso a paso 1* or *Step by Step 1*.

Supplies: None

Before you begin the class:
- Write the conversation on the board:

> **Student A:** *This is a _____*
> **Student B:** *You're right.*
> or
> **Student B:** *That isn't a _____. It's a _____ .*

How to introduce this activity
- Review objects around the classroom (*window, door, table*, etc.)
- Review the difference between *this* and *that*.
- Introduce the phrase **You're right.** (*Tienes razón.*)

Activity
- Ask a student volunteer to come to the front of the class.
- You stand close to an object, say a table, then point to it and say
> *This is a table.*
- The student says,
> *You're right.*
- Now stand close to another object, say a chair, point to it and say
> *This is a table.*
- The student says,
> *No, that isn't a table. It's a chair.*
- Point to several different objects to continue the conversation.
- Group students in pairs.
- Ask one pair to come up to the front and demonstrate.
- Students work in pairs, walking around the room and repeating the conversation.

Expansion: Repeat this activity using plural objects and *these* and *those*.

Four Corners
(Class)

Objective
- Reinforce answering short answer questions.

When to do this activity: After students have completed Section 3.7 of *Paso a paso 1* or *Step by Step 1*.

Supplies
- *Four Corners cards.* (You need enough so that each student can have one card. If you need more, make your own.)

Before the class begins
- Cut out enough cards so that each student can have one card.
- On the white board, write these sentences in large letters and evenly spaced across the length of the board.

  Yes, I am
  No, I'm not.
  Yes, she is.
  No, she isn't.
  Yes, he is.
  No, he isn't.
  Yes, it is.
  No, it isn't.
  Yes, they are.
  No, they aren't.
- If you don't have a white board, make signs and post them around the room.

How to introduce this activity
- Ask students a series of yes/no questions; then ask them to choose the correct response from the replies listed on the board.

Activity
- Give each student a card.
- Each student takes his card and stands under the appropriate sign (e.g. If your card asks *Is Michael Jordon a soccer player?*, you stand under the sign that says *No, he isn't.*)
- After students are standing under the appropriate sign, students take turns reading their cards. Other students give a *thumbs up* or *thumbs down* to indicate whether the student is standing in the correct location. If the student isn't in the correct location, they move.

Is Angelina Jolie a soccer player?	Are you tired?	Is your classroom big?	Is the moon blue?
Is Barak Obama President of Mexico?	Are you at home now?	Are the chairs in this classroom red?	Is the sun hot?
Is Barak Obama president of the United States?	Is your teacher from Guatemala?	Is today hot?	Is your sister thin?
Are your parents in the United States?	Is Michael Jordon a soccer player?	Are the students hardworking?	Is Michele Obama tall?
Is today Thursday?	Is Vicente Fernendez a singer?	Is your teacher tall?	Are your classmates from the United States?

Objective
- Reinforce how to ask questions that include the verb *to be*.

When to do this activity: After students have completed Section 3.7 of *Paso a paso 1* or *Step by Step 1*.

Supplies
- *Find 3 People*: Class set

How to introduce this activity
- Review the difference between *statements* and *questions* with the verb *to be*. Ask students to give you examples of each.
- Introduce new vocabulary: *hungry, employed, married,* and *in love*.

Activity 1
- Distribute *Find 3 People*
- Read the statement, *Find 3 people who are cooks.* Then ask students to tell you the question they'd ask a student to elicit this information, e.g. *Are you a cook?*
- Repeat this procedure for each *Find 3 People* statement. Write the questions on the board.
- Ask for a volunteer and ask them some of the questions on the worksheet. Students fill in their worksheets at the same time. <u>Make sure that students understand that they only write a classmate's name if their classmate answers the question affirmatively.</u>

Activity 2
- Students walk around the class interviewing classmates and completing their forms.
- Only write a classmate's name if he or she answers the question affirmatively.
- After students complete the form, review as a class, e.g. Ask students to look on their papers and tell you who is a cook.

 *Find 3 People*

Name _____

1. Find 3 people who are from Mexico City.

_____

_____

_____

6. Find 3 people who are cooks.

_____

_____

_____

2. Find 3 people who are married.

_____

_____

_____

7. Find 3 people who are in love.

_____

_____

_____

3. Find 3 people who are hungry.

_____

_____

_____

8. Find 3 people who are from El Salvador.

_____

_____

_____

4. Find 3 people who are employed.

_____

_____

_____

9. Find 3 people who are single.

_____

_____

_____

5. Find 3 people who are homemakers.

_____

_____

_____

10. Find 3 people who are tall.

_____

_____

_____

Conversation Practice
(Class, Tutor/Tutee)

Objectives
- Practice answering *yes/no* questions with the verb *to be.*
- Build fluency by providing an environment where students repeat the same conversation multiple times and therefore gain fluency.

When to do this activity:
- Do *Conversation Practice: Talking about yourself* after students have completed Section 3.6 of *Paso a paso 1* or *Step by Step 1.*
- Do *Conversation Practice: Talking about your brothers and sisters* and *Conversation practice: Talking about your English class,* after students have completed Section 3.7 of *Paso a paso 1* or *Step by Step 1.*

Supplies
- Class set of the *Conversation Practice* you're doing that day.

How to introduce this activity
- Introduce new vocabulary used in the conversation for that day.
- Explain that all questions are not *yes/no questions.* Ask students to give you examples of *yes/no questions* and *question word questions.* (e.g. W*hat is your name?*)

Activity
- Pass out the *Conversation Practice* worksheet and practice the conversation as a class, focusing on pronunciation. Then, ask volunteers to demonstrate.
- Students stand in two lines facing each other, line 1 and line 2.
- Student A interviews the student he's facing, Student B. Then, Student B interviews Student A.
- When students have completed their conversations, you instruct them to change partners:
  - Students in line 1 move to the right. The student at the end of the line moves to the beginning of the line.
  - Students in line 2 don't move.
- The result: Everyone has a new partner and they practice the interview again. Students stand in two lines facing each other, line 1 and line 2.

Challenge
- After students have practiced the conversation with several different partners using their papers, ask them to practice the conversation without looking at their papers.
- At the end of the activity, ask pairs of students to practice the conversation in front of the class without looking at their papers.

👥 *Conversation Practice*

Conversation Practice: Talking about yourself

Directions: When you can, answer with one of the following:

• Yes, I am.	• No, I am not.	• No, I'm not.

- How are you today?

- Are you tired?

- Are you a good student?

- Are you employed? *(empleado(a)*

- What is your job?

- Are you from the United States?

- Where are you from?

- Are you in love? *(enamorado(a)*

- Are you _____

🙂🙂 *Conversation Practice*

Conversation Practice: Talking about your brothers and sisters

Directions: When you can, answer with one of the following:

• Yes, I am.	• No, I'm not.
• Yes, he is.	• No, he isn't.
• Yes, she is.	• No, she isn't.

- I have a few questions about you and your brothers and sisters. Are you ready?
- Is your sister in the United States?
- Is your brother in the United States?
- Is your brother a student?
- Are you a student?
- Is your sister a student?
- Is your sister tall?
- Is your brother tall?
- Are you employed?
- What is your job?
- Is your sister employed?
- Is your brother employed?
- Are you healthy?
- Is your sister healthy?
- Is your brother healthy?
- Are you speaking English right now?

 # Conversation Practice

Conversation Practice: Talking about your English class

Directions: When you can, answer with one of the following:

• Yes, I am.	• No, I'm not.
• Yes, he is.	• No, he isn't.
• Yes, she is.	• No, she isn't.
• Yes, it is.	• No, it isn't.
• Yes, they are.	• No, they aren't.

- Are your classmates intelligent?

- Are your classmates lazy?

- Where are your classmates from?

- Are you a good student?

- Are you hardworking?

- Is your classroom big?

- Is your classroom clean?

- Is your teacher a woman?

- Where is your teacher from?

- Is your teacher hardworking?

Roll a Question

(Class, Tutor/Tutee)

Objective

- Build fluidity in conversation using sentence structures students are familiar with.

When to do this activity: After students have completed Chapter 3 of *Paso a paso 1* or *Step by Step 1*.

Supplies

- 1 die for every pair of students (or any size group you'd like)

Before you begin the class

- Write six questions on the board, similar to the questions students have become familiar with in class. Number the questions. Here are some suggestions:
  1. Where are you from?
  2. Are you married?
  3. Are you hungry now?
  4. Is your classroom big?
  5. What is your favorite color?
  6. What is your favorite sport?

How to introduce this activity

- Ask individual students the questions on the board.

Activity 1

- Ask for two students to demonstrate. The first student roles the die, then answers the question corresponding to the number they rolled.
- Divide students into pairs or small groups.
- Students play the game.
- If a student rolls the same number twice, they roll again.

Activity 2

- Write these six sentences on the board:
  1. Describe your brother.
  2. Describe your sister.
  3. Describe your best friend.
  4. Describe your teacher.
  5. Describe your classroom.
  6. Describe yourself.
- Repeat the game using these sentences.

Cold Turkey
(Class, Tutor/Tutee)

Objectives
- Build fluency.
- Help students gain confidence in speaking English without props.

When to do this activity: After students have completed Chapter 3 of *Paso a paso 1* or *Step by Step 1*.

Supplies: A bell or other noisemaker.

Teachers, take note: The popular Q&A site *AllExperts* dates the phrase *cold turkey* back to 1910 and states that it originally meant *without preparation*, referring to the ease of making a dish of cold turkey.

How to introduce this activity
- Ask students to ask you all of the questions they know in English. Write each one on the board. (You should have at least 20 when you're done.)
- Erase the board.

Activity
- Ask for two volunteers.
- Students come to the front of the class and converse with each other, asking and answering questions.
- Students line up in two lines facing each other.
- Student A interviews the person he's facing, Student B. Then, students switch roles.
- When you ring the bell or make some other signal, students in line 1 move to the right. The student at the end of the line moves to the beginning of the line.
- Students in line 2 don't move. The result: Everyone has a new partner and starts conversing again.

Extension
- You also can do this activity by letting students mingle and find their own partners; then, at the sound of the bell, students find a new partner to speak with.

Scrambled Sentences
(Class, Tutor/Tutee)

Objectives
- Reinforce the idea that sentences are comprised of words that can be combined in many different ways.
- Reinforce writing affirmative and negative sentences with and without contractions.

When to do this activity: After students complete Chapter 3 of *Paso a paso 1* or *Step by Step 1*.

Supplies
- *Scrambled Sentences Word Cards:* one for every two students
- *Scrambled Sentences Record Sheet* one for every two students
- Scissors for every two students

How to introduce this activity
- Review how to create affirmative and negative sentences with and without contractions.
- Introduce new vocabulary: *late, early.*

Activity
- Divide students in pairs. (Try to match students of similar ability levels. Less advanced students may only write five or six sentences while more advanced students can aim to complete their record sheets and then write more sentences on the back.)
- Give each pair a set of *Scrambled Sentence Word Cards*, a record sheet, and a pair of scissors.
- Remind students that affirmative and negative sentences go on different record sheets.
- Remind students to create some sentences with contractions and some sentences without.
- Students cut out the word cards.
- Working in pairs, students make as many sentences as they can using only the words on the card. Students record each sentence on the record sheet.
- There are more than 25 possible affirmative sentences and more than 25 possible negative sentences.
- As students finish, ask them to write one or two sentences on the board.

I	Luis	late	They're
I'm	is	early	from
not	isn't	They	Mexico
He	Laura	are	El Salvador
and	am		

Scrambled Sentences Record Sheet

Names _____

Affirmative sentences _____

1 _____

2 _____

3 _____

4 _____

5 _____

6 _____

7 _____

8 _____

9 _____

10 _____

11 _____

12 _____

13 _____

14 _____

15 _____

16 _____

17 _____

18 _____

Scrambled Sentences Record Sheet

Negative sentences

1 _____

2 _____

3 _____

4 _____

5 _____

6 _____

7 _____

8 _____

9 _____

10 _____

11 _____

12 _____

13 _____

14 _____

15 _____

16 _____

17 _____

18 _____

Teacher's Diary

Uncharted Waters

Before I wrote my own English grammar book, I spent a lot of time searching for English grammar books in Spanish that I thought would help my students. Finding a book that was thorough but not too difficult took some legwork but eventually I did find a title that I thought could be useful for more advanced students. I purchased the book and then showed it to my class. One student, Rogelio Gomez, was interested and told me that he'd pay me back if I bought the book for him. I knew that Rogelio worked as a landscaper at Stanford University so I suggested that he simply buy the book at the Stanford Bookstore. I wrote down the book's title, author and ISBN number and sent him on his way. Five minutes later he was back.

"Teacher," he implored, "Can you get the book for me?" His face suggested concern, if not outright panic.

"No problem," I replied, immediately realizing that navigating a college bookstore was not a task Rogelio was ready to take on. I respected his honesty. He could easily have pretended to go along with my suggestion, knowing full well that there was no way he was going to set foot in such alien territory. I chided myself for not realizing what a daunting feat I had asked him to undertake.

I bought Rogelio a copy of the book. He paid me for it the next day and diligently studied the book before class and during break. And at the end of the quarter he presented me with a present: a $25 gift card to the Stanford Book Store.

Objective
- To teach students to identify and spell the names of common health problems.

When to do this activity: After students have completed Section 4.1 of *Paso a paso 1* or *Step by Step 1*.

Supplies
- *Vocabulary: What's the matter?*: Class set
- Scissors for each student
- Paperclip for each student to clip their vocabulary cards

Before the class begins
- Write a list of the vocabulary words on the board:

stomachache	headache	cough	toothache
cold	fever	sore throat	backache

How to introduce this activity
- Introduce the above vocabulary by acting out each illness.
- Practice pronunciation. (*Stomachache* has got to be the most difficult word to pronounce in the English language!)
- Review when to use *have* and when to use *has*. (e.g. *I have a headache.* vs. *My brother has a sore throat.*) 1.

Activity 1
- Distribute Vocabulary Cards.
- Students cut out their cards.
- After students have cut out their cards, hold up a card and write the name of the ailment on the board. Students write the word in English <u>on the back</u> of the card.
- Do this for each card.

Activity 2
- Write this conversation on the board:

Teacher: *What's wrong with me?*
  Student: *You have a(n)* _____

- Act out an ailment and ask, *What's wrong with me?* Call on individual students to reply.

Activity 3
- Write this conversation on the board:

   Student A: *What's the matter with him? What's the matter with her?*
   Student B: *He has a* _____. *She has a* _____ .

- Explain that *him* and *her* are object pronouns that they'll learn more about in a more advanced English class. For now, all students need to understand is that *him* refers to a male and *her* refers to a female.
- Students quiz each other by showing their partner a card, then asking their partner *What's the matter with him?* or *What's the matter with her?*

Vocabulary: What's the matter?

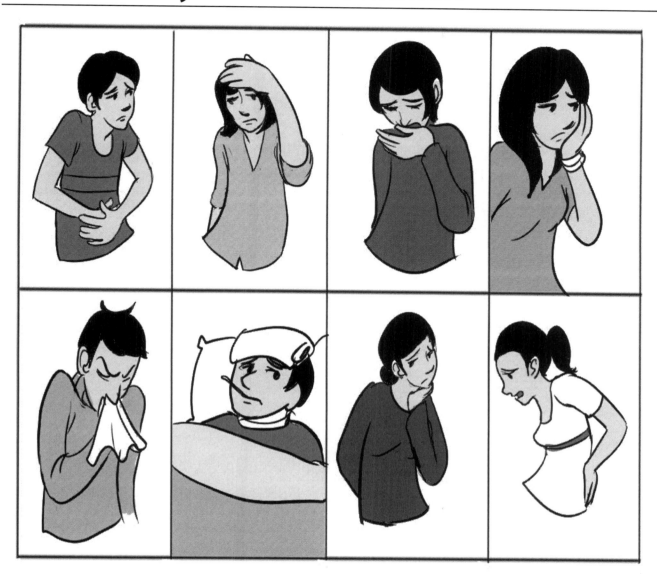

Listening Practice: Calling the clinic
(Class, Tutor/Tutee)

Objectives
- Improve listening comprehension.
- Build confidence in students' ability to write what they hear.

When to do this activity: After students have completed Section 4.1 of *Paso a paso 1* or *Step by Step 1*.

Supplies
- *Listening Practice: Calling the clinic* class set

Before the class begins:
- Choose two or three strong students and tell them you want to practice a conversation with them in front of the class. In the conversation, you are the receptionist and the student is the patient. (Conversation questions are below.) Practice the conversation a few times before class. The reply to the question, *Can I help you?* should be *I need an appointment.*

How to introduce this activity
- Introduce new vocabulary: **appointment** (*cita*).
- Introduce how to write the time in English, *3:00, 3:30, 4:00, 4:30*, etc.
- Introduce *what's* as a contraction for *what is*.

Activity
- Pass out *Listening Practice: Calling the clinic.*
- One of the volunteers you worked with before class comes to the front of the class; then you and that student practice the conversation. Students record the appropriate information on their worksheets as they listen to your conversation.
- Here are the questions you'll ask:

  Midtown Clinic, can I help you?

  What's your last name?

  Spell that please.

  What's your first name?

  Spell that please.

  What's your problem?

  Can you come to the clinic today at _____?

- Repeat the exercise with several students.
- Review the answers as a class.

Name _____

Last name	First name	Problem	Appointment time
1.			
2.			
3.			
4.			
5.			
6.			
7.			
8.			
9.			
10.			

Conversation Practice
(Class, Tutor/Tutee)

Objectives
- Provide an environment where students repeat the same conversation multiple times and thereby improve their fluency.
- Get practice making appointments and talking to medical professionals.

When to do this activity: After students have completed Section 4.1 of *Paso a paso 1* or *Step by Step 1*.

Supplies
- Class set of the *Conversation Practice* you're doing that day.

Teachers, take note: These conversations use sentence patterns that students may not have seen before. These are all common patterns that students should become familiar with, even if they don't understand the underlying grammatical structure.

How to introduce this activity
- Introduce new vocabulary used in the conversation for that day.
- Review *what's* as a contraction for *what is*.

Activity
- Pass out the *Conversation Practice* worksheet you're using that day and practice the conversation as a class, focusing on pronunciation. Then, ask two volunteers to demonstrate.
- Students line up in two lines facing each other
- Student A interviews the person he's facing, Student B. Then, students switch roles and Student B interviews Student A.
- Students in line 1 move to the right. The student at the end of the line moves to the beginning of the line.
- Students in line 2 don't move. The result: Everyone has a new partner and practices the interview again.

Challenge
- After students have practiced the conversation with several different partners, ask them to practice the conversation without looking at their papers.
- At the end of the activity, ask pairs of students to practice the conversation in front of the class without using their papers.

Conversation Practice

Conversation Practice: Making a doctor's appointment

Receptionist: Can I help you?

Patient: I need an appointment with the doctor.

Receptionist: What's the matter?

Patient: I have a _____

Receptionist: What's your last name?

Patient: My last name is _____

Receptionist: What's your first name?

Patient: My first name is _____.

Receptionist: Are you available today at _____?

Patient: Yes, _____ _____

Receptionist: OK. See you later.

Patient: Thank you very much.

Receptionist: You're welcome.

✏️ Conversation Practice

Conversation Practice: Talking to the doctor

Doctor: Good afternoon. How are you feeling?

Patient: I'm very sick.

Doctor: What's the matter?

Patient: I have a _____

Doctor: Anything else?

Patient: I have a _____

Doctor: Do you have a fever?

Patient: Yes, I do.

Doctor: Are you taking medicine?

Patient: Yes, I'm taking _____

Doctor: OK. I will examine you now.

 **Conversation Practice**

Conversation Practice: Picking up a prescription

Pharmacist: Can I help you?

Patient: I need to pick up a prescription.

Pharmacist: What's your last name?

Patient: _____

Pharmacist: Spell that please.

Patient: _____

Pharmacist: What's your first name?

Patient: _____

Pharmacist: What's your telephone number?

Patient: _____

Pharmacist: Who is your doctor?

Patient: My doctor is Dr. _____.

Pharmacist: Here is your prescription.

Patient: Thanks very much.

Pharmacist: You're welcome. Have a nice day.

Double Dictation: Plurals
(Class, Tutor/Tutee)

Objective
- Give students practice spelling and pronouncing singular and plural nouns, with an emphasis on irregular plural nouns.

When to do this activity: After students complete Section 4.4 of *Paso a paso 1* or *Step by Step 1*.

Supplies
- *Double Dictation: Plurals:* One copy for every two students

Before the class begins
- Cut each worksheet in half horizontally. One student will have the *Student A* worksheet and his partner will have the *Student B* worksheet.

How to introduce this activity
- Write a list of singular nouns on the board. including irregular single nouns (*man, woman, child, tooth,* and *foot.*) Ask students to pronounce each singular noun; then pronounce and spell its plural form. Pay particular attention to the pronunciation of *man, men, woman,* and *women.* Explain that in both cases the *a* changes to an *e*.

Activity
- Divide students into pairs.
- Give one member of each pair the Student A worksheet and one member the Student B worksheet.
- Ask for a volunteer to read the directions on the worksheet.
- Clarify the assignment:
  - Student A reads her word list to Student B. Student B writes the words on the right side of her form.
  - Student B reads her word list to Student A. Student A writes the words on the right side of her form.
- Explain that, after both partners have dictated their words, they should check to make sure they've spelled the words correctly.

Double Dictation: Plurals

Name _____

Student A: Read these words to your partner.	Student A: Write the words your partner reads to you.
1. woman	1. _____
2. women	2. _____
3. kiss	3. _____
4. kisses	4. _____
5. boys	5. _____
6. boy	6. _____
7. teeth	7. _____
8. tooth	8. _____
9. children	9. _____
10. child	10. _____
Student B: Read these words to your partner.	Student B: Write the words your partner reads to you.
1. man	1. _____
2. men	2. _____
3. toy	3. _____
4. toys	4. _____
5. people	5. _____
6. person	6. _____
7. class	7. _____
8. classes	8. _____
9. foot	9. _____
10. feet	10. _____

Scrambled Sentences
(Class, Tutor/Tutee)

Objectives
- Reinforce the notion that sentences are comprised of words that can be combined in many different ways.
- Reinforce when to use *have* and when to use *has*.

When to do this activity: After students complete Section 4.5 of *Paso a paso 1* or *Step by Step 1*.

Supplies
- *Scrambled Sentences Word Cards:* one for every two students
- *Scrambled Sentences Record Sheet* one for every two students
- Scissors for every two students

How to introduce this activity
- Review when to use *has* and when to use *have*.
- Review where to place adjectives (*before* the noun).
- Review when to use *a* and when to use *an*.

Activity
- Divide students in pairs. (Try to match students of similar ability levels. Less advanced students may only write five or six sentences while more advanced students can aim to complete their record sheets and then write more sentences on the back.)
- Give each pair a set of *Scrambled Sentence Word Cards*, a record sheet, and a pair of scissors.
- Students cut out the word cards.
- Working in pairs, students make as many sentences as they can using only the words on their cards. Students record each sentence on the record sheet.
- There are more than 25 possible sentences.
- As students finish, ask them to write one or two sentences on the board.

✍ *Scrambled Sentences Word Cards*

Erica	Julian	new	car
has	a	house	old
and	have	They	We
She	He	an	I

 Scrambled Sentences Record Sheet

Names_____

1 _____

2 _____

3 _____

4 _____

5 _____

6 _____

7 _____

8 _____

9 _____

10 _____

11 _____

12 _____

13 _____

14 _____

15 _____

16 _____

17 _____

18 _____

19 _____

20 _____

Objectives
- To encourage students to write what they hear.
- To teach students some frequently-used phrases.

When to do this activity: After students have completed Section 4.5 of *Paso a paso 1* or *Step by Step 1*.

Supplies:
- Each student needs a piece of paper, or they can write in their notebooks.

Before class begin: Write this on the board:

Ana: _____ _____. _____ _____ _____?
Mario: *Not so good.*
Ana: _____ _____ _____ _____?
Mario: ____ _____ _____ _____ _____
Ana: *I'm sorry. I hope you feel better.*
Mario: _____ _____

Activity
- Read the following conversation, one line at a time. Students write what you read. Encourage students to say *Spell that please.* (The second and sixth line are already written since they include many new words.)
  Ana: *Hi Mario. How are you?*
  Mario: *Not so good.*
  Ana: *What is the matter?*
  Mario: *I have a bad headache.*
  Ana: *I'm sorry. I hope you feel better.*
  Mario: *Thank you.*
- Teach any new vocabulary as you go.
- Dictate the conversation a second time.
- Walk around and check students' papers.
- Ask students to come to the board to write individual lines of the conversation.
- Practice the conversation as a class, with the men reading Mario's part and the women reading Ana's part.
- Ask individual students to take the parts of Ana and Mario and "perform" the conversation.
- Delete *headache* and have students substitute their own ailments.
- Ask students to practice the conversation in pairs.

Extension: Create your own dictation conversations! Students really like this activity, And it's great practice since it includes listening, writing, and speaking.

Four Corners
(Class)

Objective
- Reinforce answering short answer questions.

When to do this activity: After students have completed Section 4.7 of *Paso a paso 1* or *Step by Step 1*.

Supplies
- *Four Corners cards.* (You need enough so that each student has one. If you need more, make your own.)

Before the class begins
- Cut out enough cards so that each student has one.
- On the white board, write

  have

  has

  am

  is

  are
- If you don't have a white board, make signs and post them around the room.

How to introduce this activity
- Review when to use the verb *to be* and when to use *have* and *has*.

Activity
- Give each student a card.
- Each student takes his card and stands under the appropriate sign (e.g. If your card says *I _____ 23 years old*, you stand under the sign that says *am*.)
- After students are standing under the appropriate sign, students take turns reading their cards. Other students give a *thumbs up* or *thumbs down* to indicate whether the student is standing in the correct location. If the student isn't in the correct location, they move.

📖 Four Corners

We _____ two children.	Laura and I _____ students.	I _____ three children.	We _____ from Peru.
I _____ tired.	He _____ my brother.	They _____ from Michoacan.	Andrew _____ at work.
We _____ sick.	My sister _____ 22 years old.	The students _____ late.	I _____ hungry.
We _____ a new car.	I _____ a cold.	Javiar _____ a computer.	I _____ a good job.
My child _____ a sore throat.	Lourdes _____ two children.	My daughter _____ a good teacher.	My mother _____ brown eyes.

Classmate Interviews: *How old are you?*

(Class)

Objectives
- Build fluency by providing an environment where students can easily converse with each other.
- Reinforce the use of *have* to talk about age.

When to do this activity: After students have completed Section 4.7 of *Paso a paso 1* or *Step by Step 1*.

Supplies
- *Classmate Interviews: How old are you?* Class set

How to introduce this activity
- Ask students how old they are. Then ask students how old their classmates are (e.g. *Maria, how old are you? Class, how old is Maria?*)
- Remind students that they don't have to tell the truth when asked their age and that, in general, it's not considered polite to ask anyone over twenty how old they are.
- As a review, ask students what job they have.

Activity
- Distribute a copy of *Classmate Interviews: How old are you?* to each student.
- Display a copy so everyone can see it, or copy the conversation on the board.
- Read the conversation, with students repeating each line after you read it.
- Ask for two student volunteers, one to ask the questions and one to answer them. The volunteers interview each other. Students who are seated record the results of these interviews on their interview form.
- Students move around the class interviewing fellow students and completing their forms.
- After everyone has completed their interviews, ask students about their peers, e.g. *How old is Miguel? What is Alex' job?*

👥 *Classmate Interviews: How old are you?*

Name _____

Person A: What's your name?

Person B: My name is _____

Person A: Spell that please.

Person B: _____

Person A: What's your job?

Person B: I'm a(n) _____

Person A: How old are you?

Person B: I'm _____ years old.

Person A: Thanks for your time.

Person B: You're welcome.

Name	Job	Age
1.		
2.		
3.		
4.		
5.		
6.		
7.		
8.		
9.		
10.		

Find 3 People: *Do you have...*
(Class)

Objective
- Introduce the construction *Do you have...* and the responses: *Yes, I do,* or *No, I don't.*

When to do this activity: After students have completed Section 4.7 of *Paso a paso 1* or *Step by Step 1.*

Supplies
- *Find 3 People: Do you have...*: Class set

Teachers, take note: Using *do* and *does* correctly is one of the most challenging aspects of learning English. This topic is taught in depth in *Paso a paso 2* and *Step by Step 2.* However, simply teaching students to use *Do you have* as a way of asking questions, then replying *Yes, I do,* or *No, I don't,* is definitely a reasonable expectation given all that students have learned thus far.

How to introduce this activity
- Write the following on the board:
  - *Do you have a car?*
    - *Yes, I do.*
    - *No, I don't.*
  - *Do you have a job?*
    - *Yes, I do.*
    - *No, I don't.*
- Practice answering these and similar questions that start with *Do you have...*
- Review the difference between *statements* and *questions* that include the verb *to have.* Ask students to give you examples of each.

Activity 1
- Distribute *Find 3 People: Do you have...*
- Read the statement, *Find 3 people who have a job.* Then ask students to tell you the question they'd ask a student to elicit this information, e.g. *Do you have a job?*
- Repeat this procedure for each *Find 3 People* statement. Write the corresponding question on the board.
- Ask a volunteer some of the questions on the worksheet. Students fill in their worksheets accordingly. <u>Make sure that students understand that they only write a classmate's name if their classmate answers the question affirmatively.</u>

Activity 2
- Students walk around the class interviewing classmates and completing their forms.
- Only write a classmate's name if they answer the question "Yes".
- After students complete the form, review as a class, e.g. Ask students to check their papers and tell you who has a job.

☺☺ Find 3 People: Do you have...

Name _____

1. Find 3 people who have a job. ——————————————— ——————————————— ———————————	6. Find 3 people who have a sister in the United States. ——————————————— ——————————————— ———————————
2. Find 3 people who have a TV in the kitchen. ——————————————— ——————————————— ———————————	7. Find 3 people who have a bicycle. ——————————————— ——————————————— ———————————
3. Find 3 people who have a computer. ——————————————— ——————————————— ———————————	8. Find 3 people who have a backpack. ——————————————— ——————————————— ———————————
4. Find 3 people who have family in the United States. ——————————————— ——————————————— ———————————	9. Find 3 people who have a cell phone. ——————————————— ——————————————— ———————————
5. Find 3 people who have a brother in the United States. ——————————————— ——————————————— ———————————	10. Find 3 people who have children. ——————————————— ——————————————— ———————————

Objectives
- Introduce the construction *Do you like...*, and *Do you need...*, and the responses: *Yes, I do,* or *No, I don't.*
- Review how to ask questions that start *Do you have...*

When to do this activity: After students have completed Section 4.7 of *Paso a paso 1* or *Step by Step 1.*

Supplies
- *Find 3 People: Do you like...*: Class set

Teachers, take note: This lesson builds on the previous one. Although using *do* and *does* is taught in depth in *Paso a paso 2* and *Step by Step 2,* the constructions *Do you have...*, *Do you need...* and *Do you like...* are useful expressions for students to learn now.

How to introduce this activity
- Review the difference between *statements* and *questions* with the verb *to have*. Ask students to give you examples of each.
- Write the following on the board:
  - *Do you need a computer?*
    - *Yes, I do.*
    - *No, I don't.*
  - *Do you like to play soccer?*
    - *Yes, I do.*
    - *No, I don't.*
  - *Do you have a car?*
    - *Yes, I do.*
    - *No, I don't.*
- Practice answering these and other similar questions.

Activity 1
- Distribute *Find 3 People: Do you like...*
- Read the statement, *Find 3 people who like salsa music.* Then ask students to tell you the question they'd ask a student to elicit this information, e.g. *Do you like salsa music?*
- Repeat this procedure for each *Find 3 People* statement. Write each question on the board.
- Ask a volunteer some of the questions on the worksheet. Students fill in their worksheets accordingly. Make sure that students understand that they only write a classmate's name if their classmate answers the question affirmatively.

Activity 2
- Students walk around the class interviewing classmates and completing their forms.
- After students complete the form, review as a class, e.g. Ask students to look on their papers and tell you who likes chocolate.

👥👥 *Find 3 People, Do you like...*

Name _____

1. Find 3 people who like pizza. _____ _____ _____	6. Find 3 people who need a new job. _____ _____ _____
2. Find 3 people who like salsa music. _____ _____ _____	7. Find 3 people who need a car. _____ _____ _____
3. Find 3 people who like chocolate. _____ _____ _____	8. Find 3 people who like to play soccer. _____ _____ _____
4. Find 3 people who have a computer. _____ _____ _____	9. Find 3 people who have family in the US. _____ _____ _____
5. Find 3 people who have a cell phone. _____ _____ _____	10. Find 3 people who like to study English. _____ _____ _____

Two Halves Make a Whole
(Class, Tutor/Tutee)

Objective
- Help students distinguish between when to use *to have* and when to use *to be.*

When to do this activity: After students have completed Section 4.7 of *Paso a paso 1* or *Step by Step 1.*

Supplies:
- *Two halves make a whole* worksheet: one copy for every two students
- Scissors for every two students

How to introduce this activity
- Review when to use *have* and when to use *to be.*
  - *To have*: For possessions and to state your age.
  - *To be*: To describe people, to state your occupation, to say where you're from.
- Review sentences like *I am hungry, I am thirsty,* and *I am 22 years old,* since these use a different verb in English than in Spanish.

Activity
- Divide students in pairs.
- Give each pair a pair of scissors and the handout.
- Ask for a volunteer to read the directions on the worksheet.
- Students cut out the sentence fragments. They should have 20.
- Students make correct sentences by putting two strips together. There is more than one way to match the sentence fragments.
- Once you've checked students' sentences, they should record them on their worksheets. This reinforces what they have learned.

Extension: Have students make their own sentence strips!

✍ Two Halves Make a Whole

Name _____

Directions: Cut out each rectangle. You should have twenty rectangles. Then, make correct sentences. Write your sentences on the record sheet.

I	are husband and wife.
Roberto	have three children.
Miguel and Thomas	has a beautiful garden.
Ana and Margarita	are brothers.
You	is a teacher.
Alberto	is 32 years old.
Ana and Raymundo	are very late.
Laura	are sisters.
Clara and Guillermo	has a new car.
Martha	is thirsty.

Record sheet

1.
2.
3.
4.
5.
6.
7.
8.
9.
10.

Teacher's Diary

The Invisible

It's the last week of class and my students are taking their final exams. All have finished, except for one. At the time, I can't even remember her name. She's plump and 30ish, with a touch of mestizo that reminds me of how stunning she must have been ten years ago. She is wearing a white shirt with red embroidery across the top that fits a bit too snugly and sandals that are a tad too small for her plump feet. When she walks, she bows her head. Everything about her says, "Don't notice me, please," and I realize that unknowingly, I followed that direction. But when she hands me her exam, she lingers and we start to talk. She's from Guatemala. She's been here ten years. She has a son who is five. And, oh yes, she also has a son in Guatemala. He's ten. She left him when he was one. Her mother takes care of him. Her son's teacher tells her mother that the boy is such a good student that he's in charge of raising the flag.

Before her younger son was born, she had two jobs; she was a prep cook at a fancy Italian restaurant and she cleaned houses. But now she devotes all of her time to her son. He speaks English with her and corrects her. "We are going to the store," she tells me he tells her. And I imagine a five year old who already has figured out how to be in charge of his Mom. The best thing that has happened to her since the birth of her son is that she can drive. Her husband told her he'd give her exactly three driving lessons. Fortunately, she was a quick study. I know she doesn't have a license—few of my students do—which makes driving at least as stressful as it is liberating, but I don't mention that.

Her husband is a manager of janitors. He speaks English well. In fact, he learned a lot of it at our school. But he isn't home much. She doesn't have a lot of friends. I ask whether she goes to church. No, she doesn't go to church. On Saturdays she does the wash. On Sundays she cleans her apartment.

She looks at the clock, not realizing how long she has been talking, and turns to leave. Spontaneously, I give her a hug. I'll probably never see her again but, for those ten minutes we connected in a way that I haven't connected with people I've know a thousand times as long, only because she wanted to talk and I wanted to listen. As she walks away, I remember her name. It is Delela.

Vocabulary: Clothes
(Class, Tutor/Tutee)

Objective
- To teach students to identify and spell the names of articles of clothing.

When to do this activity: After students have completed Section 5.1 of *Paso a paso 1* or *Step by Step 1*.

Supplies
- *Vocabulary: Clothes:* Class set
- Scissors for each student
- Paperclip for each student to clip their vocabulary cards

Before the class begins: Make sure you can identify each drawing: *jacket, shoes, socks, pants, shirt, sweatshirt, earrings, necklace, hat, blouse, dress, coat*

How to introduce this activity
- Point to various articles of clothing and ask students to identify them.

Activity: Part 1
- Distribute Vocabulary Cards.
- Students cut out their cards.
- After students have cut out their cards, hold up a card and write what it is on the board. Students write the word in English <u>on the back</u> of the card.
- Do this for each card.

Activity: Part 2
- Divide students in pairs.
- Ask students which items are singular (*jacket, shirt, sweatshirt, necklace, blouse, hat, dress, coat*) and which words are plural (*shoes, socks, pants*). On the board, make two lists: one with the singular items and one with the plural items.
- Write this conversation on the board:

  Student A: *What is this?*

  Student B: *It is a _____.*

  Student A: *Spell that please.*

  Student B: _____.

- Write this conversation on the board:

  Student A: *What are these?*

  Student B: *They are _____.*

  Student A: *Spell that please.*

  Student B: _____

- Practice these conversation as a class, making sure students know when to use each one.
- Students practice these conversations with their partners, showing their partner a vocabulary card; then asking their partner to identify the item shown and spell it.

Vocabulary: Clothes

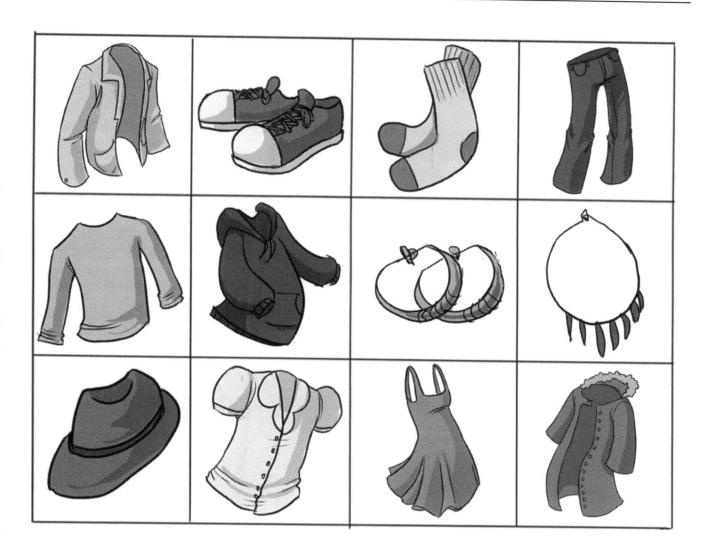

Talking about your classmates
(Class)

Objectives
- Practice using *his* and *her*.

When to do this activity: After students have completed Section 5.2 of *Paso a paso 1* or *Step by Step 1*.

Supplies
- *Talking about Your Classmates:* Class set.

How to introduce this activity
- Talk about when to use *is* and *are* with clothes, e.g. *His shirt is blue. His pants are black.*
- Explain that *He has black hair* and *His hair is black* mean the same thing.

Activity
- Ask a student to come to the front of the class. This is Student 1. Write his/her name on the worksheet.
- Students write four sentences about the person. At least two should begin with *his/her*, e.g., *His hair is brown, His eyes are black, His shirt is red,* etc.
- Ask several students to read their sentences about Student 1.
- Repeat this procedure for each student.

👥 *Talking About Your Classmates*

Name _____

Directions: Write four sentences about each student.

Student 1's Name _____
1._____
2. _____
3. _____
4. _____

Student 2's Name _____
1._____
2. _____
3. _____
4. _____

Student 3's Name _____
1._____
2. _____
3. _____
4. _____

Student 4's Name _____
1._____
2. _____
3. _____
4. _____

Student 5's Name _____
1._____ _____
2. _____
3. _____
4. _____

Picture 6's Name _____
1._____
2. _____
3. _____
4. _____

Line Up!

(Class)

Objective
- Practice knowing when to use *his* and when to use *her*.

When to do this activity: After students have completed Section 5.2 of *Paso a paso 1* or *Step by Step 1*.

Supplies
- none

How to introduce this activity
- Ask a student *What is your name?* Then, pointing to that student, ask another student *What is her name?*
- Repeat this activity with several students.

Activity 1
- Ask students to stand in a straight line in from of the classroom.
- Each student, in turn, states their first name, for example, "*My name is _____*. Tell students to pay attention since they're going to have to try to repeat the names of each student.
- Ask for a volunteer to go down the line and identify each of his classmates using the sentences, *His name is _____* or *Her name is _____*
- The first student who can correctly identify each student and correctly use the possessive pronouns *his* and *her* is the winner.

Extension
- You can do the same type of lineup for a host of different questions, such as
  - *Where are you from?*
  - *When is your birthday?*
  - *How old are you?*

Photo Share
(Class, Tutor/Tutee)

Objectives
- Build fluency.
- Help students gain confidence in speaking English without props.

When to do this activity: After students have completed Section 5.2 of *Paso a paso 1* or *Step by Step 1*.

Supplies: None

A few days before you plan to do this activity: Ask students to bring in photographs of their family members.

How to introduce this activity
- Introduce some family vocabulary that students may not know: **aunt** (*tía*), **uncle** (*tío*), **cousin** (*primo, prima*), **grandmother** (*abuala*), **grandfather** (*abuelo*).

Activity
- Ask for a volunteer to bring their photo to the front of the classroom. Tape it to the board or pass it around.
- With your help, students ask the student with the photo questions about who is in the picture, e.g.
  - *Who is that?*
  - *What is his name?*
  - *Where is he now?*
  - *What is his job?*

Extension: Students write a short description of their family member.
- Cut out pictures of people from magazines for students who didn't bring in a photo.
- Do a sample story as a class and write it on the board. For example:

  > *This is Marcos Rivera. He is my uncle. He is 22 years old. He is from Mexico. His hair is long. His eyes are blue. He has a blue shirt.*

- Students write their own stories, then glue them to a piece of paper along with their photo.
- Post the stories and photos.

Objectives
- Build fluency by providing an environment where students can easily converse with each other.
- Reinforce the use of *his* and *her*.

When to do this activity: After students have completed Section 5.2 of *Paso a paso 1* or *Step by Step 1*.

Supplies
- *Classmate Interviews: What is your sister's name?* Class set

Teachers, take note: Possessive nouns don't exist in Spanish. Instead, *your sister's name* translates, literally, to *the name of your sister (el nombre de tu hermana)*. Students learn this in *Paso a paso 2*.

How to introduce this activity
- Ask students *What is your sister's name?* and W*hat is your brother's name?* They should reply using the *his name is/her name is* construction.
- Explains that *sister's* is a possessive noun, that Spanish doesn't have possessive nouns and that students will learn about possessive nouns in *Paso a Paso 2*.

Activity
- Distribute a copy of *Classmate Interviews: What is your sister's name?* to each student.
- Display a copy of the worksheet so everyone can see it, or copy the conversation on the board.
- Read the conversation, with students repeating each line after you read it.
- Ask for two student volunteers, one to ask the questions and one to answer them. The volunteers interview each other. Students who are seated record the results of these interviews on their interview form.
- Remind students to say *I don't have a sister* or *I don't have a brother* where appropriate.
- Students move around the class interviewing fellow students and completing their forms.
- After everyone has completed their interviews, ask students about their peers, e.g. *What is the name of Jose's sister?*

😀😃 Classmate Interviews: *What is your sister's name?*

Name _____

Person A: What is your name?

Person B: My name is _____

Person A: Spell that please.

Person B: _____

Person A: What is your sister's name?

Person B: Her name is _____

Person A: What is your brother's name?

Person B: _____ name is _____.

Person A: Thanks for your time.

Person B: You're welcome.

Name	Sister's name	Brother's name
1.		
2.		
3.		
4.		
5.		
6.		
7.		
8.		
9.		
10.		

Conversation Practice

(Class, Tutor/Tutee)

Objectives
- Get practice making appointments and talking to medical professionals.
- Provide an environment where students repeat the same conversation multiple times and thereby improve their fluency.

When to do this activity: After students have completed Section 5.2 of *Paso a paso 1* or *Step by Step 1*.

Supplies
- Class set of the *Conversation Practice* you're doing that day.

How to introduce this activity
- Review how to answer yes/no questions.
- Review when to use *his* and *he* and *her* and *she*.

Activity
- Pass out the *Conversation Practice* worksheet and practice the conversation as a class, focusing on pronunciation. Then, ask two volunteers to demonstrate.
- Students line up in two lines facing each other
- Student A interviews the person he's facing, Student B. Then, students switch roles and Student B interviews Student A.
- Students in line 1 move to the right. The student at the end of the line moves to the beginning of the line.
- Students in line 2 don't move. The result: Everyone has a new partner and they practice the interview again.

Challenge
- After students have practiced the conversation with several different partners, ask them to practice the conversation without looking at their papers.
- At the end of the activity, ask pairs of students to practice the conversation in front of the class without using their papers.

😃😃 Conversation Practice

Student A: What is your sister's name?

Student B: Her name is _____

Student A: What color is your sister's hair?

Student B: Her hair is _____

Student A: What color are your sister's eyes?

Student B: Her eyes are _____

Student A: Is your sister tall?

Student B: _____ _____ _____

Student A: Is your sister in the US?

Student B: _____ _____ _____

Student A: What is your brother's name?

Student B: His name is _____

Student A: What color is your brother's hair?

Student B: His hair is _____

Student A: What color are your brother's eyes?

Student B: _____

Student A: Is your brother heavy?

Student B: _____ _____ _____

Student A: Is your brother in your country now?

Student B: _____ _____ _____

Telephone

(Class)

Objectives
- Reinforce when to use *your* and when to use *his* and *her*. This is extremely confusing for beginning students!

When to do this activity: After students have completed Section 5.3 of *Paso a paso 1* **or** *Step by Step 1*.

Supplies
- *Telephone:* Class set

Before the class begins
- Make three large signs and post them around the room, as far away from each other as possible. The first sign should say *Speakers;* the second sign should say *Runners;* the third sign should say *Writers.*

How to introduce this activity
- Introduce new vocabulary: **speaker** *(hablador(a)),* **runner** *(corredor(a)),* **writer** *(escritor(a).*
- Play a game of Telephone: Five students come to the front of the class and sit in a line. Whisper an English sentence in the ear of the first person in the line. That person repeats the sentence to the next person. This continues down the line. The final person says the sentence out loud to the class.
- Explain that students are going to do an activity very similar to Telephone using possessive pronouns.

Activity
- Give each student a copy of the *Telephone* worksheet.
- Divide students into groups of three. Assign each person in the group a job: *Speaker, Runner,* or *Writer.*
- Each student goes to the correct location in the classroom (e.g. *Speakers* stand under the *Speakers* sign, *Runners* stand under the *Runners* sign, etc.)
- Explain that only the *Writers* need their worksheets. Students in other groups will use their worksheet later.
- Demonstrate the activity with one group of students, who do the following:
  - The Runner goes to the Speaker and asks, *What is your last name?*
  - The Speaker replies, for example, *My last name is Gomez.*
  - The Runner says, *Spell that please,* if necessary.
  - The Runner goes to the Writer and says *His last name is Gomez.*
  - The Writer records this information on his worksheet.
  - The Runner goes back to the Speaker and asks, *What is your address?*
  - The Speaker replies, for example, *My address is 25 5th Ave.* The Runner goes to the writer and says, *His address is 25 5th Ave.*
- This continues until the Writer's *Telephone* worksheet is complete.
- Students switch roles and repeat the exercise.
- Students reconvene in their groups of three to check each other's work for accuracy.

🔊 *Telephone*

Name _____

Directions: Answer these questions. Use a complete sentence.

1. What is the speaker's last name?

2. . What is the speaker's address?

3. What is the speaker's job?

4. What is the speaker's favorite sport?

5. What is the speaker's favorite kind of pizza?

Listening Practice
(Class, Tutor/tutee)

Objectives
- Improve listening comprehension.
- Build confidence in students' ability to distinguish between pronouns and possessive adjectives.

When to do this activity: After students have completed Section 5.4 of *Paso a paso 1* or *Step by Step 1*.

Supplies
- *Listening Practice:* class set

How to introduce this activity
- Review the difference between *he* and *him, she* and *her,* and *they* and *their, it* and *its.*

Activity
- Pass out *Listening Practice.*
- Read the paragraph. Students write the missing word on their worksheets.

   Paragraph 1
   My uncle's name is Roberto. **He** is married. **His** wife is Anthelma. **They** have two children. **Their** children are Alfredo and Jessica. **They** are good children but **they** are very noisy. When **I** go to **their** house, **I** get a headache.

   Paragraph 2
   My aunt has two dogs. **Her** big dog is black and white. **His** name is Gonzo. **Her** small dog is Bobo. Bobo is brown. **My** aunt also has a fish. **Its** name is Swimmy.

   Paragraph 3
   I am a waiter. **I** like my job. **My** boss is a good person. **His** name is Hector. **He** speaks only English. **His** wife also works at the restaurant. **She** is a cook. **They** have three children. Sometimes **their** children come to the restaurant.

   Paragraph 4
   Luciano is **my** best friend. **He** is friendly and hardworking. **He** lives in Texas with **his** wife. **Luciano** is tall and thin. **His** eyes are blue and **his** hair is blonde. **His** wife is Laura. **She** is short and heavy. **Her** hair is black and **her** eyes are black. **They** are opposites. But **they** are in love.

- Read again.
- Review as a class.

✨)) *Listening Practice*

Name_____

Directions: Listen to your teacher read the paragraph. Fill in the missing words.

Paragraph 1

My uncle's name is Roberto. _____ is married. _____ wife is Anthelma. _____ have two children. _____ children are Alfredo and Jessica. _____ are good children but _____ are very noisy. When _____ go to _____ house, _____ get a headache.

Paragraph 2

_____ aunt has two dogs. _____ big dog is black and white. _____ name is Gonzo. ___ small dog is Bobo. Bobo is brown. _____ aunt also has a fish. _____ name is Swimmy.

Paragraph 3

_____ am a waiter. _____ like _____ job. _____ boss is a good person. _____ name is Hector. _____ speaks only English. _____ wife also works at the restaurant. _____ is a cook. _____ have three children. Sometimes _____ children come to the restaurant.

Paragraph 4

Luciano _____ my best friend. _____ is friendly and hardworking. _____ lives in Texas with _____ wife. Luciano is tall and thin. _____ eyes are blue and _____ hair is blonde. _____ wife is Laura. _____ is short and heavy. _____ hair is black and _____ eyes are black. _____ are opposites. But _____ are in love.

Conversation Dictation
(Class, Tutor/Tutee)

Objectives
- To encourage students to write what they hear.
- To teach students some frequently-used phrases.

When to do this activity: After students have completed Section 5.4 of *Paso a paso 1* or *Step by Step 1*.

Supplies:
- Each student needs a piece of paper or they can write in their notebook.

Before class begins: Write this on the board:

Mario: _____ _____ _____ _____ _____?
Ana: _____ _____ _____ _____.
Mario: _____ _____ _____?
Ana: _____ _____ _____ _____ _____. _____ _____ _____ _____ _____.
Mario: _____ _____ _____?
Ana: _____ _____ _____ _____ _____ _____ _____ _____ _____
_____ _____.
Mario: _____ _____ _____?
Ana: _____ _____ _____.
Mario: _____ _____ _____.

Activity
- Read the following conversation, one line at a time. Students write what you read. Encourage students to say *Spell that please.*

  Mario: *What is your sister's name?*
  Ana: *Her name is Karla.*
  Mario: *Is she pretty?*
  Ana: *Yes, she is very pretty. She is tall and thin.*
  Mario: *Is she intelligent?*
  Ana: *Yes, she is very intelligent and she has a very good job.*
  Mario: *Is she married?*
  Ana: *Yes, she is.*
  Mario: *That's too bad.*

- Walk around and check students' papers.
- Ask students to come to the board to write individual lines of the conversation.
- Practice the conversation as a class, with the men reading Mario's part and the women reading Ana's part.
- Ask individual students to take the parts of Ana and Mario and "perform" the conversation.
- Ask students to practice the conversation in pairs at their seats.

Objectives
- Practice using the possessive adjectives *my, his, her, our,* and *their.*
- Teach the difference between *in* and *from.*
- Reinforce using the verb *to be.*

When to do this activity: After students complete Chapter 5 of *Paso a paso 1* or *Step by Step 1.*

Supplies
- *Scrambled Sentences Word Cards:* one for every two students
- *Scrambled Sentences Record Sheet* one for every two students
- Scissors for every two students

How to introduce this activity
- Teach students the difference between *in* (I am <u>in</u> Mexico.) and *from* (I am <u>from</u> Mexico.)
- Reinforce the use of possessive adjectives. Focus on *their* and *our.*

Activity
- Divide students in pairs. (Try to match students of similar ability levels. Less advanced students may only write five or six sentences while more advanced students can aim to complete their record sheets and then write more sentences on the back.)
- Give each pair a set of *Scrambled Sentence Word Cards*, a record sheet, and a pair of scissors.
- Remind students to create some sentences with contractions and some sentences without.
- Students cut out the word cards.
- Working in pairs, students make as many sentences as they can using only the words on their cards. Students record each sentence on the record sheet.
- There are more than 25 possible sentences.
- As students finish, ask them to write one or two sentences on the board.

My	Your	His	Her
Their	Our	uncle	brothers
parents	is	are	from
Mexico	Nicaragua	in	friends

✍ *Scrambled Sentences Record Sheet*

Names_____

1 _____

2 _____

3 _____

4 _____

5 _____

6 _____

7 _____

8 _____

9 _____

10 _____

11 _____

12 _____

13 _____

14 _____

15 _____

16 _____

17 _____

18 _____

19 _____

20 _____

Four Corners

(Class)

Objective
- Reinforce answering short answer questions.

When to do this activity: After students have completed Chapter 5 of *Paso a paso 1* or *Step by Step 1*.

Supplies
- *Four Corners cards.* (You need enough so that each student has one. If you need more, make your own.)

Before the class begins
- Cut out enough cards so that each student has one.
- On the white board, write, across the length of the board,

    my
    your
    his
    her
    our
    their
    its

- If you don't have a white board, make signs and post them around the room.

How to introduce this activity
- Review when to use each of the possessive pronouns above.

Activity
- Give each student a card. Note that many cards include unfamiliar words. Have them look these words up in their dictionary, then share the meaning of the new words with the class.
- Each student takes his card and stands under the appropriate sign (e.g. If your card says Y*ou are very tall. _____ daughter is tall too*, you stand under the sign that says *your*.)
- After students are standing under the appropriate sign, students take turns reading their cards. Other students give a *thumbs up* or *thumbs down* to indicate whether the student is standing in the correct location. If the student isn't in the correct location, they move.

👥👥 Four Corners

We have two daughters. _____ daughters are in Mexico.	My sister is tall. ____ daughter is tall too.	I am tired today. ____ head hurts.	Susan has a new baby. _____ baby is beautiful.
My husband and I have two children. _____ children like to play soccer.	Luis and Maria are my friends. _____ house is near my house.	I like my job. _____ boss is a good person.	Andrew has a good job. _____ salary is very high.
I have a daughter. _____ name is Caroline.	I have a small house. _____ house has only three rooms.	I have two daughters. _____ names are Chelsea and Caroline.	We are happy but _____ children are sad. They want to go back to Mexico.
You are very tall. _____ children are tall too.	My sister is beautiful. _____ hair is black and _____ eyes are black too.	My brother is very intelligent and _____ wife is very intelligent too.	You are a good student. _____ parents are very lucky!
My dog is crazy. _____ name is Loco.	My cat is very thin. _____ name is Delgadita.	Mario has a beautiful garden. _____ garden has many trees.	Ana has a fish. ____ name is Bobo.

Resources for Beginning ESL Students

If you've been unable to find clear, well thought out ESL books for Spanish-speaking students in the very beginning stages of learning English, you're not alone. That said, there are some quality resources you should know about. Here they are, along with where to find them. Note that prices may change and Web site have been known to vanish.

Where to buy ESL books

Spring Book Center: (http://www.springesl.com/cart/). The best place to purchase ESL books online is Spring Book Center. The collection is extensive and the owner, Luis Coloma, extremely knowledgeable about the vast array of ESL materials available. Feel free to call him at (866) 431-1199. Tell him your needs and he'll recommend appropriate texts.

Pro Lingua Books: http://www.prolinguaassociates.com/ This is large publisher of ESL texts for all levels that aren't necessarily available at other sites.

Amazon: www.amazon.com. A vast numbers of ESL books are available here. Plus, you often can get great deals on used books.

Reading books

Gianola, Ann, *Easy Stories Plus*, Syracuse, New York: New Readers Press, 2000. ISBN 9781564202529, $11.75. Easy stories, somewhat predictable but engaging nonetheless. Each story is followed by comprehension, grammar, and vocabulary exercises.

Heyer, Sandra, *Very Easy True Stories, A Picture-Based First Reader,* White Plains, NY: Addison Wesley, Longman, 1998. ISBN 978-0201343137, $23.95. High interest stories taken from real life. Stories are easy to follow due to drawings that depict plots as they unfold. Each story is followed by exercises.

Books in Spanish that teach English

Harvey, William C., *Inglés para Latinos,* New York: Barrons, 2003. ISBN 978-0764119903, $10.99. This book is more like a warm blanket than a text. While it's short on substance, it may make Spanish speakers less intimidated about trying to learn English due to the author's breezy style, cooky illustrations and practical advise (For example, *No olvides que está bien mezclar los dos idiomas si no te acuerdas de la palabra apropiada. Remember it's ok to mix both languages if you forget the appropriate word.*). It also includes useful vocabulary and some rudimentary, though incomplete, grammar explanations.

Levenson, Ana I., *Gramática Española para estudiantes de Inglés,* Ann Arbor, Michigan: Olivia & Hill Press, 1993. ISBN 97809793034173. $19.95. The idea behind this book is that it will be easier to understand English grammar if you also understand Spanish grammar. While it won't have much appeal for the casual learner, curious students who find grammar intrinsically interesting will find the relatively simple explanations useful.

Harvey, William C., *Ingles para todos los días,* New York, Barrons,
ISBN 978-0764175305, $16.95. Even though this book is intended for children. it
includes lots of useful vocabulary and pithy grammar tips.

Audio materials:

Pimsleur English for Spanish Speakers: Level 1. ISBN 978-0671784768. This exclusively
audio way of learning English is extremely effective, particularly for audio as opposed
to visual learners. Includes sixteen hours of spoken instruction. It's expensive but lots
of libraries carry it. You also can get used copies fairly cheaply online.

Bilingual dictionaries

Many beginning students will find electronic translators far more useful than
dictionaries since they eliminate the time and agony associated with looking up
words. For students who can't afford a translator, both of the dictionaries below are
useful, though very different.

Lipton, Gladys C., Munoz, *Spanish-English/English-Spanish Beginner's Dictionary*
Olivia, NY: Barrons, 2009, ISBN 978-0764139680, $8.99. A real beginner's dictionary,
with only a few words per page. The definitions are short and easy to understand.

Oxford Picture Dictionary: English/Spanish. Oxford University Press, USA; 2nd
edition, 2008. 978-0194740098, $17.95. Features more than 4,000 words and phrases
in English and Spanish, illustrated with vivid artwork.

Web sites

- http://www.usalearns.org/index/intro/index.html A fantastic, free site with
  extensive videos, plus supplementary materials. Available with explanations in
  Spanish.
- inglesmundial.com An expansive site intended for Spanish speakers.
- http://www.pdictionary.com/ The Internet picture dictionary
- http://www.manythings.org/lulu/ Easy vocabulary games.
- http://www.eslfast.com/easydialogs/ Good listening practice.